ESCAPE LONDON

DAYS OUT WITHIN EASY REACH OF LONDON

YOLANDA ZAPPATERRA

PHOTOGRAPHS BY KIM LIGHTBODY

FF

FRANCES
LINCOLN

CONTENTS

INTRODUCTION

As any of its natives or adopted sons and daughters will tell you, London is one of the greatest cities in the world. It has a rich culture and history, vast open spaces, cutting-edge architecture and countless lovely Londoners. Perhaps best of all though, it has incredible access to some of the best day-trip destinations in Britain.

Beyond the suburbs, in every direction, lie cultural, gastronomic and historical jewels in a region where human habitation stretches back at least 800,000 years. Over time, eccentric individuals and innovative communities have come together to create a wealth of unique and idiosyncratic attractions that can be enjoyed to this day. And all are nestled in a beloved landscape of chalk downs and rolling hills, stunning beaches and dappled forests, magnificent gardens and glistening waterways. It's an embarrassment of riches in every sense. In such abundance, there is truly something for everyone – a day trip to suit every mood, whatever the weather and whatever your age.

From the hundreds of towns, villages and attractions within some 90 minutes of the capital, I've cherry-picked 30 of the best. Featuring well-known favourites alongside some unexpected treats, the destinations feature a range of activities that will make whichever day trip you take unforgettable. I hope you have as much fun visiting them as I did.

CULTURE & HERITAGE

LAVENHAM

You'd be forgiven for thinking you had just walked onto the set of a period costume drama when first entering Lavenham; the Suffolk village is a perfect snapshot from the medieval era and there are very few places in Britain quite like it. But this is no film-set fakery; Lavenham gained its market charter from Henry III in 1257 and has a wonderfully rich history. Elizabeth I is said to have dropped by on royal progress in 1578 with an entourage of hundreds of servants, and Romantic painter John Constable came to study here 200 years later. Let's gloss over the town's torrid reputation (in centuries past, public executions and bull baiting had been regular occurrences here), and focus on Lavenham's charm, which once enticed John Lennon and Yoko Ono to take a hot-air balloon from the Market Square. The pair most likely, as everybody else does, fell under the spell of the lime-washed, brightly coloured buildings around them, of which 340 are listed. Must-sees include: the Corpus Christi Guildhall (Market Lane), used in the past as a prison and workhouse but now acting as the village museum and tearoom; the De Vere House (Water Street, pictured left), which starred in *Harry Potter and the Deathly Hallows* as the young wizard's birthplace; and the numerous shops on High Street. If it's raining, Merchants Row at the junction of Church Street and Water Street has a cluster of independent shops that neatly capture the spirit and architecture of this handsome village.

—

Get there: *Trains run from London Liverpool Street to Sudbury, seven miles away, taking around 80 minutes. From there, the number 753 bus runs to Lavenham.*

✤ THE PARISH CHURCH OF ST PETER & ST PAUL

Looking more like a cathedral than a church, this late-medieval masterpiece has some outstanding features including a wealth of carving in oak and stone and incredible stained glass windows. The church is open daily, though you may have to dodge the odd wedding. Call ahead to confirm access or arrange a guided tour.

—

Church Street, CO10 9SA.
01787 247244
www.lavenhamchurch.wordpress.com

❖ LAVENHAM FALCONRY AT MONKS ELEIGH

If the medieval settings inspire you to partake in some age-old activities, head for this fantastic falconry just four miles outside the village. A range of activities and experiences include a two-hour hawk walk or owl handling, as well as full-day falconry sessions, eagle flying and archery.

—

Corncraft, Bridge Farm Barns,
Hadleigh Road, Monks Eleigh, IP7 7AY.
01787 249691
www.lavenhamfalconry.co.uk

❖ SWAN HOTEL

The Airmen's Bar at the Swan Hotel is a great pit stop for a pint or a bite to eat, although you may end up staying longer than planned thanks to its fascinating interior filled with all manner of things to take in. You might linger over the Royal Air Force memorabilia and a wall signed by British and American air force personnel who were stationed at the nearby airfield during the Second World War.

—

High Street, CO10 9QA.
01787 247477
www.theswanatlavenham.co.uk

❧ THE ANGEL

For a spot of tea or a light lunch try the cosy Munnings Tea Room (7 High Street). For something more fancy, the French-owned Great House (Market Place) is undoubtedly Lavenham's most elegant restaurant. But for down-home, traditional food The Angel is a real crowd-pleaser – its thoughtfully crafted seasonal menu features delicious lamb and game from the nearby Denham Estate.

Market Place, CO10 9QZ.
01787 247388
www.theangellavenham.co.uk

❧ LAVENHAM LITTLE HALL

The seven rooms of this late fourteenth-century hall are home to a winning range of art and artefacts that provide a nice introduction to the history and development of the village and its architecture, as well as domestic medieval living. The gardens are gorgeous too, featuring a traditional rose garden and a Tudor inspired knot-garden.

Market Place, CO10 9QZ.
01787 247109
www.littlehall.org.uk

AUDLEY END HOUSE & GARDENS

The Essex village of Saffron Walden is a true jewel on London's periphery, a market town that has managed to retain its own distinct identity but also move with the times to present a welcoming, appealing face to visitors. Cheery shopkeepers and friendly locals are clearly proud of their town and the only problem you're likely to have on a day trip here is fitting everything in, especially as the must-do attraction will take up at least two to three hours. The Jacobean mansion Audley End House (pictured left) has been much remodelled since its almost total destruction in the late 1600s, and it's fun trying to identify the different periods of building inside. But it's the outside that's the real draw: the gardens, largely designed in the eighteenth century by Capability Brown, feature natural planting, a serpentine lake and a colourful restored parterre. Small but distinct spaces reveal something new at every turn; the Kitchen Garden sees peonies and irises bump heads with veggies and crowing chickens, while the Pond Garden features dazzling seasonal displays, and sculptural trees stand proud in the Elysian Garden. With elegant buildings designed by Robert Adam dotted throughout the gardens, the grounds make for an exciting visit at any time of year – a perfect London escape.

—

Audley End, Saffron Walden, Essex, CB11 4JF.
01799 522842, www.english-heritage.org.uk/audleyend

Get there: *Trains run from London Liverpool Sreet to Audley End Station, one-and-a-half miles away, taking around one hour. From there, a five-minute taxi ride will take you to the House & Gardens.*

❖ EXPLORE SAFFRON WALDEN

Cameras at the ready for the impossibly cute, brightly coloured, half-timbered terraced cottages along Castle Street, the huge Parish Church of St Mary (visible for miles), and the largest turf maze in Britain. Finish up with a picnic in the gorgeous Bridge End Gardens, a series of seven interlinked gardens laid out in the nineteenth century.

❖ THE FRY ART GALLERY

As regional galleries go, The Fry must be one of the
best. Its permanent collection of works produced
by the Great Bardfield creative community of
the early twentieth century includes hundreds
of pieces by Edward Bawden, Eric Ravilious and
Michael Rothenstein. These are rotated so
that each visit is different, with temporary
exhibitions further adding to the gallery's appeal.

Castle Street, Saffron Walden, CB10 1BD.
01799 513779
www.fryartgallery.org

❖ SAFFRON WALDEN MUSEUM

This family-friendly social history museum is full of unexpected and occasionally surreal objects that will appeal to all ages. Mummy cases, woolly mammoths and the remains of food and clothing from a prehistoric Swiss village are just a few of them. Nearby, the castle ruins are fun to explore and a meadow acts as a peaceful spot for a packed lunch.

—

Museum Street, Saffron Walden, CB10 1JL.
01799 510333
www.saffronwaldenmuseum.swmuseumsoc.org.uk

❖ THE EIGHT BELLS

Stripped pine boards, winged armchairs and Chesterfield sofas make this watering hole ideal for a day-trip timeout. And it's but a stone's throw from the Fry Gallery (see page 19) and Saffron Walden Museum (see opposite). If you're hungry, sit in the sixteenth-century barn and pretend you're at a Tudor feast, or if it's just a drink you're after, head to the sunny deck outdoors.

—

18 Bridge Street, Saffron Walden, CB10 1BU.
01799 522790
www.8bells-pub.co.uk

❖ THE CHEDDAR VINE

This wine shop and deli is home to more than 100 New World wines and 45 different British cheeses. Enjoy some of the latter alongside a varied selection of pâtés, antipasti and salumi as part of a delicious lunch platter. Six miles away, the sixteenth-century Cricketers at Clavering (Wicken Road) also serves excellent food courtesy of Jamie Oliver's parents, Trevor and Sally.

—

8A Cross Street, Saffron Walden, CB10 1EX.
01799 523853
www.thecheddarvine.com

TUDELEY CHURCH

The French pride themselves on Matisse's fabulous stained glass windows at the Chapelle du Rosaire de Vence, but a parish in Kent can lay claim to a whole church full of one artist's stained glass work. The tiny All Saints' Church in Tudeley is the only church in the world whose stained glass windows (pictured left) are all designed by Marc Chagall. The contrast between the humble church and the rich European modernism of the artist's swirling blues and golds is unmissable. This surreal duality begins even before you step inside the church, which spans two centuries and many different materials – the unusual, square, red-brick tower looks determinedly modern in contrast to the sandstone nave, but it was actually built in 1765. Once inside the space is harmoniously unified by Chagall's twelve resplendent windows, commissioned in 1963 after the tragic death of young modern art lover Sarah d'Avigdor-Goldsmid. Her parents asked Chagall to design the large east window as a tribute to their daughter, but on arriving in 1967 to install the window Chagall apparently said: 'It's magnificent. I will do them all.' Colours range from golden yellows to deep blues via bursts of orange, purple and pink, and detailed scenes encompass traditional Chagall tropes of hope and joy, such as angels, asses, birds and horses. Experiencing them all here in this very special little church is truly magical.

—

All Saints' Church, Tudeley, Tonbridge, Kent, TN11 0NZ.
01892 833241, www.tudeley.org

Get there: *Trains run from London Bridge to Tonbridge, two and a half miles away, taking around 45 minutes. From there, the number 205 bus runs to the church, or you can hire a bike in Tonbridge.*

✤ CHURCH OF ST THOMAS À BECKET

Just a 20-minute walk from All Saints' Church, the captivating Norman Wealden Church of St Thomas à Becket (Church Lane, Five Oak Green, Capel) also holds some artistic merit – thirteenth-century wall paintings decorate most of the nave. Seven miles away, St Mary's Speldhurst (Southfields) has notable stained glass windows by Edward Burne-Jones and William Morris.

Church Lane, Capel, Five Oak Green, Tonbridge, TN12 6SX. www.tudeley.org/stthomasbecketcapel.htm

❧ THE POACHER & PARTRIDGE

Another short walk from All Saints' Church, this smart pub is light, spacious and surrounded by lots of terrace seating outside. An eclectic menu ensures something for all tastes and budgets. And if you've yet to take a walk in the area, you'll find plenty of helpful information on hand here.

Hartlake Road, Tudeley, Tonbridge, TN11 0PH.
01732 358934
www.elitepubs.com/poacher_partridge

♣ BIKE RIDE TO PENSHURST PLACE

A purpose-built countryside cycle route – the Tudor Trail – links Tonbridge Castle (see opposite) with Penshurst Place, a fortified manor house with meticulously pruned gardens. If they look familiar, it might be because both starred in the BBC adaptation of *Wolf Hall*. The nearby Penshurst village is sweet too and its church features another arresting stained glass window by Lawrence Lee.

—

Cycle-Ops, Bank Street, Tonbridge, TN9 1BL.
01732 500533
www.cycle-ops.co.uk/hire

❧ RSPB TUDELEY WOODS

If you come to this beguiling mix of woodland and heathland in spring, you'll walk through a glorious carpet of primroses, wood violets and bluebells. If you come in autumn, you'll find more than a thousand species of fungi. But come year-round to see and hear the stars of the show: the birds. Among them is Britain's rarest breeding woodpecker species, rather appropriately named the 'lesser spotted' woodpecker.

—

Half Moon Lane, Tonbridge.

01273 775333

www.rspb.org.uk

❧ TONBRIDGE CASTLE

Thanks to two large-scale restoration projects undertaken in the early 2000s, the remains of this thirteenth-century motte-and-bailey gatehouse are surprisingly intact and extremely evocative. An entertaining, hour-long audioguide takes you past interactive displays and life-size figures on a fascinating journey through 900 years of British history. The surrounding lawns and gardens also make a top picnic spot.

—

Castle Street, Tonbridge, TN9 1BG.

01732 770929

www.tonbridgecastle.org

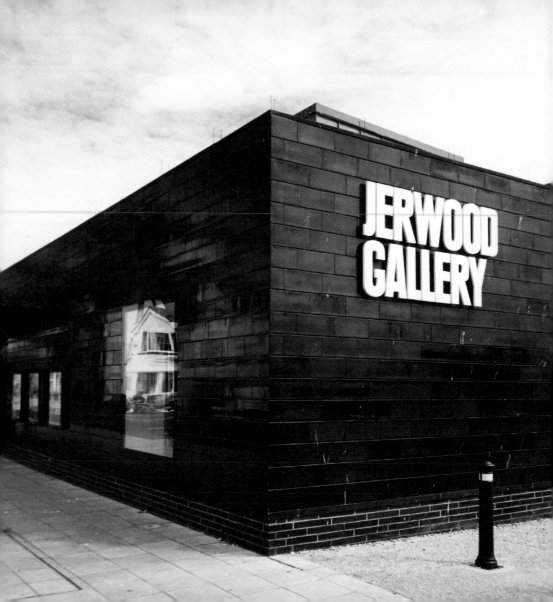

HASTINGS

For a long time, Hastings was the unwelcome guest at the South Coast party, more shabby than shabby-chic. But over the last few years it has become a go-to destination for tourists, with an eclectic mix of indie shops, pubs, bars, galleries and restaurants – just make sure you find you way to George Street and High Street where gift stores, antique shops and cafés jostle for attention. The twisting twittens of these Old Town roads lead variously to the lavish stained glass windows of St Clements Church (Croft Road), the glorious double-height fishermen's huts of the old fishing harbour and the swanky 910-foot pier, renovated just last year with 42 miles of hardwood decking. For the more artistic, the new Printworks Art Club (14 Claremont) hosts a number of events and the Jerwood Gallery (Rock-a-Nore Road, pictured left) is home to an impressive collection of contemporary British art. And if you weren't already spoilt for choice, just one stop after Hastings on the train down from London is the charming St Leonards-on-Sea – jump off at St Leonards Warrior Square and rifle through old records and knick-knacks at the antique and charity shops, or sample the delights of wine merchant Phoenix & Plum (Kings Road). For a tea break, head to one of a handful of cafés close to the seafront; Michaela's Cute Cakes (London Road), The Love Café (28 Norman Road) and Smiths (21 Grand Parade) all come highly recommended. There's enough on this little stretch of coast to make an overnight stay highly recommended and, nowadays, enough cute little B&Bs and hotels that will make you glad you did.

—

Get there: *Trains run from London St Pancras International with a change at Ashford, taking around 90 minutes.*

✤ HASTINGS COUNTRY PARK

After a morning exploring the streets of the Old Town, clear your head and lungs with an exhilarating walk in 345 hectares of ancient woodland and heathland bordered by three miles of dramatic cliffs and a coastline dotted with hidden coves and waterfalls. Take the funicular railway or brave the five-minute climb.

—

East Hill Lift, Rock-A-Nore Road, TN34 3EG.
01424 451111
www.visit1066country.com

❖ FIRST IN LAST OUT

Hastings has a pub to suit all tastes, but beer fans and pub traditionalists should beat a path to the friendly, laidback First In Last Out. Six home-brewed ales are served in an old-school space complete with board games and live music. Grab a cosy corner in one of the wooden booths and enjoy good food in great company. Pub nirvana.

—

14–15 High Street, Old Town, TN34 3EY.
01424 425079
www.thefilo.co.uk

❖ ST CLEMENT'S

For delicious traditional fish dishes, the Rock-A-Nore Kitchen in Hastings (23 Rock-A-Nore Road) will not disappoint. But for a more refined meal head to St Leonards-on-Sea where chef patron Nick Hales's St Clement's has a deserved Michelin Bib Gourmand for its modern British food dished up in a warm, rustic space.

—

3 Mercatoria, St Leonards-on-Sea, TN38 0EB.
01424 200355
www.stclementsrestaurant.co.uk

❖ HASTINGS MUSEUM & ART GALLERY

Long before the Jerwood Gallery arrived, this museum was quietly pleasing visitors with its peculiar mix of Mods and Rockers photos, nineteenth-century smugglers exhibits and the bizarre Durbar Hall, constructed for the Indian and Colonial Exhibition of 1886. It couldn't be more different to the Jerwood, but it's just as good.

Johns Place, Bohemia Road, TN34 1ET.
01424 451052
www.hmag.org.uk

❖ BEXHILL-ON-SEA

Five miles east along the coast from Hastings, Bexhill-on-Sea has all the seaside resort essentials plus one standout attraction: the stunning 1935 modernist De La Warr Pavilion on the Marina (pictured bottom right), now a national centre for contemporary arts. Petrol-heads might prefer the Motoring Heritage Centre (Banbury Road) and others the refurbished Bexhill Museum (Egerton Road, pictured top right) focusing on local history.

ARUNDEL

Arundel's pristine station is a very fine introduction to this very fine market town, including as it does a waiting room furnished with leather sofas and bookshelves filled with paperbacks. Heading north from the station, the South Downs spread out like a luscious carpet of rolling hills bordered by the River Arun, which marks the southern edge of Arundel's old town, just a ten-minute walk away. The town continues the arty mien of the station with an eclectic selection of independent shops. Vinyl records can be found at A Ray of Delight (12 The Old Printing Works, Tarrant Street), antiques, arts and crafts at Ninevah House (31 Tarrant Street), and walking sticks at, yes, The Walking Stick Shop (8–9 The Old Printing Works, Tarrant Street). Perhaps the best of the stores is the Victorian warehouse of Sparks Yard (18 Tarrant Street), which fills two floors with a winning mix of homeware and gifts and whose bright and spacious third floor houses The Loft – a California-inspired restaurant that provides great food alongside great views of the town. Fortified, it's time to head to this town's top attraction: Arundel Castle, arguably one of the South-East's finest (its gardens are pictured left). If you've time after that, end the day with one of a range of country walks in and around the town: one of these weaves past Swanbourne Lake and Lodge in the 1,000-acre Arundel Park, another through the ruins of a medieval priory, and many more delve deep into the sprawling South Downs National Park.

—

Get there: *Trains run direct from London Victoria, taking around 90 minutes.*

✤ ARUNDEL CASTLE

The eleventh-century Arundel Castle has been home to the Dukes of Norfolk for centuries, and is a day trip in its own right. But if you're pressed for time, highlights include the art collection (which contains works by Gainsborough and Van Dyck), the fountains, pavilions and mountain of The Collector Earl's Garden, and the medieval tapestries and workmanship of the castle's interior.

—

BN18 9AB.

01903 882173

www.arundelcastle.org

✣ ROMAN CATHOLIC CATHEDRAL OF OUR LADY & ST PHILIP HOWARD

Were it not for the castle, Arundel's cathedral would be the standout structure in town. Built in a French Gothic style, but dating back to the 1870s, its grand spires loom over the Tudor and Georgian buildings below. A short but steep climb from the centre of town, the delicate rose window and striking west façade are definitely worth the effort.

London Road, BN18 9AY.
01903 882297
www.arundelcathedral.org

❖ WWT ARUNDEL WETLAND CENTRE

There are plenty of satisfying walks to be had in and around Arundel, but if you've little ones in tow or want some guaranteed encounters with the natural world, the Wetland Centre is ideal. Activities include boat safaris, bird feeding and pond dipping, but a simple walk through the hushed reed beds listening to nothing but the wind and the wildlife is pure bliss.

Mill Road, BN18 9PB.
01903 883355
www.wwt.org.uk/wetland-centres/arundel

❖ BLACK RABBIT

Its riverside location with masses of waterside seating, fantastic views of the castle, good range of ales and ciders and traditional pub food make the Black Rabbit a top spot for lunch or a restorative pint after a nice country walk. The pub recommends a relaxed three-mile round trip from its doors that takes you north along the banks of the river up to the small hamlet of South Stoke and back down through quiet lanes to the comfort of your second pint.

———

Mill Road, BN18 9PB.
01903 882828
www.theblackrabbitarundel.co.uk

❖ THE WATERSIDE TEA GARDEN AND BISTRO

For a traditional cream tea with homemade scones, this riverside bistro takes the biscuit. But it also serves a terrific range of meals and snacks, many homemade using locally sourced produce. Speciality breads, pizzas and signature wood-smoked dried tomatoes are cooked in a wood-fire oven and the menu is updated daily depending on the catches of fishermen in nearby Worthing. Local fare at its freshest.

———

Mill Road, BN18 9PA.
01903 882609
www.thewatersidearundel.co.uk

COOKHAM

Wandering through the settings of an artist's oeuvre is always fascinating and doing so in as picturesque a place as the Berkshire village of Cookham is a delight. Sir Stanley Spencer lived here for most of his life and depicted many of the village's features in paintings such as *Pound Field*, *Englefield House*, *Bellrope Meadow* and *The Garden at Cookham Rise*. It's huge fun to explore the village and nearby countryside finding the spots from which he painted these and numerous other landscapes. The excellent Stanley Spencer Gallery (see overleaf) has a full-colour booklet detailing three walks between half an hour and 90 minutes long that will help you do just that. But the village itself also has much to enjoy, not least the enduring Norman features of the Holy Trinity Church and the cherry orchards at Cookham Dean, a village once home to *Wind in the Willows* author Kenneth Grahame. Further afield lies Enid Blyton's childhood home of Old Thatch, Bourne End, which is now closed to visitors, but which still makes for a nice three-mile round walk from the village. Though perhaps best of all is the proximity of the village to the Thames: its attendant riverside meadows gradually give way to chalk downland, providing yet more walking opportunities as well as an inspiring landscape from which to try your own sketches and paintings.

—

Get there: *Trains run from London Paddington to Cookham with a change at Maidenhead, taking around one hour in total.*

❖ STANLEY SPENCER GALLERY

Behind an unprepossessing white façade, the Stanley Spencer Gallery holds a huge collection of the artist's paintings and drawings. From his *Cookham Regatta* series to rural landscapes and domestic scenes, the breadth of work and style is fascinating and is sure to set you off around the village in search of his painting posts.

High Street, SL6 9SJ.
01628 471885
www.stanleyspencer.org.uk

❖ VILLAGE WALK

The easiest of the three walks listed in the Spencer Gallery's booklet is a 30-minute ramble past the artist's childhood home and some of his most important landmarks, including the Holy Trinity churchyard that appears in his *Resurrection* series. Here you'll find the beautiful stone angel statue painted by Spencer as well as a memorial stone marking the centenary of Spencer's birth.

❖ BEL & THE DRAGON

Don't expect cosy, dark nooks and crannies in this Tudor coaching inn dating from 1417. This is a determinedly bright and breezy gastropub with a contemporary feel. An open kitchen allows diners to watch the chefs in action and the wine list includes its very own white and red Burgundies made under licence by wine estate Olivier Leflaive.

—

High Street, SL6 9SQ.
01628 521263
www.belandthedragon-cookham.co.uk

❖ CLIVEDEN

The gardens overlooking the Thames here are spectacular, particularly in the spring when the 30,000 bulbs and plants planted in the parterre create a lush carpet of colour. The Long Garden, Water Garden and recently restored Rose Garden are just as striking, while the woodlands and maze are fun places for little ones to let off some steam.

Cliveden Road, Taplow, Maidenhead, SL1 8NS.
01628 605069
www.nationaltrust.org.uk/cliveden

❖ THE TEAPOT TEA SHOP

The old-school service and fare — homemade cakes, crumpets and toasted teacakes — set in a fresh and bright space make this a most appealing venue for an afternoon break. Owners Diane and Magda also serve brunch and lunch, with gluten-free options included. Be sure to grab a local Beechdean Farmhouse Dairy ice cream for pudding.

1–2 Clieve Cottages, SL6 9SJ.
01628 529514
www.teapot-teashop.co.uk

45

GARDENS & GREENERY

WALTHAM ABBEY

To stroll through Waltham Abbey's market square today is to walk in the footsteps of Roman soldiers and Saxon kings in a settlement dating back more than 2,000 years. With its sweet village feel, it's hard to imagine you're just half an hour away from the heart of London, and in the grounds of Waltham Abbey Church (pictured left) you'll feel even further away from modern life. A gateway with separate arches for carts and pedestrians dates back to the fourteenth century, a medieval bridge fords the Cornmill Stream and behind the church itself, a stone slab marks the supposed grave of the last Saxon king, Harold, famously killed in 1066 at the Battle of Hastings. Both the town and the church palpably resonate with these monumental moments in British history in a parkland setting that includes a rose garden, riverside walks and lots of sites for picnicking. The Abbey Gardens give way to the Abbey fishponds and, less than a mile beyond them, the wildlife haven of Cornmill Meadows – a wetland area that supports a wide variety of dragonflies, damselflies and birds, all visible from a hide. Both the gardens and fishponds are part of the Lee Valley Park, which stretches for 23 miles along the River Lee in a string of wetlands, waterways and nature reserves, and which is home to more than 30 walks. And all of it is free!

—

Get here: *Trains run from London Liverpool Street to Waltham Cross, just over a mile away, taking around half an hour.*

❖ WALTHAM ABBEY CHURCH

The last resting place of King Harold is a medieval gem. The elegant rounded Norman nave arches meet a muralled ceiling adorned with zodiacal figures that is topped only by the chancel stained glass windows designed by Edward Burne-Jones. A free leaflet gives lots of insight into the church's features – the Imps of Waltham are particularly charming.

—

Abbey Gardens, EN9 1XQ.
01992 767897
www.walthamabbeychurch.co.uk

✤ COPPED HALL

Just four miles outside town, this eighteenth-century Palladian mansion under restoration is a fascinating work in progress and includes the largest walled garden in the county. Guided tours of the house and gardens take place on the third Sunday of every month (except December) and an open garden day is held on the first Sunday of each month from April to September.

—

Crown Hill, Epping, CM16 5HS.
07799 473108
www.coppedhalltrust.org.uk

❖ THE EPPING FOREST DISTRICT MUSEUM

Occupying a handsome Grade II-listed Tudor building, this newly refurbished museum relays the story of the district through absorbing exhibits and activities for curious children. In the new Core Gallery, key pieces from the museum's extensive collection are shown on a rotating basis.

—

39–41 Sun Street, EP9 1EL.
01992 716882
www.eppingforestdc.gov.uk/index.php/out-and-about/museums/museum-home

❖ THE WELSH HARP

Backing directly onto Abbey Gardens, the Welsh Harp is Waltham Abbey's only medieval inn and the tables outside its lopsided timber-framed front make a fine spot for a pint in the sun. It serves a good range of food from noon–4pm, including favourites such as homemade steak and ale pie with mash. And it's all very affordable.

—

Market Square, EN9 1DL.
01992 711113
www.mcmullens.co.uk/welsh-harp

✤ TONY'S PIE & MASH

This being Essex, it would be quite remiss not to head down to this local favourite and eat a plate of the county's most famous food export. But if you really can't abide eels, then the quaint garden setting and more accessible fare of Philpott's Tea Rooms in nearby Lynchgate House (Church Street, just behind Waltham Abbey Church) may be more appealing.

—

7–8 Market Square, EN9 1DP.
01992 652798

SISSINGHURST CASTLE & GARDENS

All too often, stately gardens are attached to stately homes with all the attendant stately grandeur… Parterre? Check. Rose garden? Check. Huge mixed borders? Check. They're glorious, but sometimes much of a muchness in their planting and design. Sissinghurst is a refreshingly individualistic exception. Created in the 1930s by the writer and poet Vita Sackville-West and her husband Harold Nicolson, the gardens' abundant, romantic mix is a treat. It includes, among others, a cottage garden, purple border, herb garden, lime walk, nuttery, orchard and white garden (the most famous of all). Each achieves a gentle harmony with the other and the rich red-brick buildings of the castle. The castle itself dates from the sixteenth century and before Vita and Harold purchased the 450-acre estate in 1930, it saw service both as a prison for French soldiers during the Seven Years' War and as a home to the Women's Land Army, a civilian organisation created during the World Wars to boost the depleted agricultural workforce. Indoors, the dramatic double-turreted tower (pictured left) and brimming library shouldn't be missed, the latter for its 11,000 books and art deco furnishings and the former for Vita's own cosy study, a small exhibition space and, best of all, rooftop views of the estate – it's from here you can see just how neatly all the buildings, gardens and wider estate connect.

—

Biddenden Road, near Cranbrook, Kent, TN17 2AB.
01580 710700, www.nationaltrust.org.uk/sissinghurst-castle-garden

Get there: *Trains run from London Charing Cross to Staplehurst, five miles away, taking around one hour. From there, the number 5 bus goes within a mile of the Castle & Gardens, or you can download a cycle route from the National Trust's website.*

❧ CRANBROOK MUSEUM

In a building made up of four fifteenth-century timber-framed listed cottages, Cranbrook Museum has the kind of exhibits and ephemera that appeal to the collector in all of us. A huge collection of stuffed birds sits alongside hundreds of works of art by members of the creative Cranbrook Colony, which painted local scenes from 1854 onwards. A strange but rewarding mix.

Carriers Road, Cranbrook, TN17 3JX.
01580 712929
www.cranbrookmuseum.org

❖ THE MILK HOUSE

The sixteenth-century Milk House has a relaxed, convivial atmosphere and a good range of hand pump ales along with a nicely varied selection of food. Its huge flagstone terrace is a prime location for a pint and a pizza, cooked in the outdoor oven during summer months.

The Street, Sissinghurst, TN17 2JG.
01580 720200
www.themilkhouse.co.uk

❖ THE HIGH WEALD LANDSCAPE TRAIL

The 90-mile-long High Weald Landscape Trail from Horsham to Rye passes by Cranbrook, where a three-mile circular walk following part of it through woodland and farmland starts near the White Horse Inn (Carriers Road). There's a shorter walk to Sissinghurst Castle too, one of a selection in the area organised by Kent County Council.

—

www.kent.gov.uk/explorekent

❖ THE THREE CHIMNEYS

Decreed Kent's best dining pub of 2015 by the Good Pub Guide, this fifteenth-century waterhole is a real winner. Depending on your mood, there are five different eating areas to choose from: head to the extension overlooking the garden for formal dining, the gardens themselves if the weather holds out, or the main restaurant for a casual meal. Wherever you choose, the food is pretty special.

—

Hareplain Road, Biddenden, TN27 8LW.
01580 291472
www.thethreechimneys.co.uk

❖ CRANBROOK

The wooden weatherboard-clad buildings and hilly streets of Cranbook are ideal for an hour's exploration, and the shopping here is fantastic. For gifts, head to Spice (5 Stone Street) and Maisie K (23 Stone Street), or one of the many well-stocked charity shops. For treats, pop to old-school sweetshop The Sweet Train (Stone Street) or family bakers Chaney & Son (High Street). Need a break? The Waterloo House Tea Rooms (1 Waterloo Road) should do the trick.

RYE

Hanging baskets filled with vibrant tumbling colours, black-beamed medieval houses and clambering cobbled streets with far-reaching views across Romney Marsh make Rye one of the prettiest towns on the South Coast – but it's not all about the looks. This thirteenth-century Cinque Port has an engaging history with past residents ranging from wool smugglers to notable authors such as authors Henry James and E F Benson; the latter used Rye as the basis for the fictional town of Tilling in his *Mapp and Lucia* books. It's perhaps this fact more than any other that began to draw visitors here in the first half of the twentieth century, but it's the friendliness of the locals – many of them still employed in a thriving commercial fishing fleet – alongside the terrific antique and vintage shops and top notch pubs and restaurants that keep them coming back. These days, the tourists often outnumber the locals, but the town manages to retain a homely, down-to-earth feel that extends even to its top attraction, Lamb House. Here, fans of E F Benson's gently humorous tales can explore the original home of the writer and fictional home of Miss Mapp while amiably rubbing shoulders with more serious literary bods looking for the inspiration behind Henry James's more tortured oeuvre. Though they'll be lucky to find anything, as there's nothing remotely torturous about Rye, unless perhaps you hate hanging baskets.

—

Get there: *Trains run from London St Pancras International with a change at Ashford, taking around one hour in total.*

❖ YPRES CASTLE INN

Rye is home to more than its fair share of first-rate pubs, with The Standard Inn (33 The Mint) and the white clapboard Globe Inn Marsh (10 Military Road) on the outskirts of town among them. But it's the seventeenth-century Ypres Castle Inn that stands out, with a great garden and even greater views from its perch beneath the ruined castle's ramparts.

—

Gungardens, TN31 7HH.
01797 223248
www.yprescastleinn.co.uk

❖ NEW 2 YOU RETRO

It's almost unfair to single out any one shop in Rye; there are a huge number to choose from and pretty much all of them have something for everyone. New 2 You focuses on twentieth-century clothing and homeware, while a few doors away Bidgoods (52 Cinque Ports) specialises in nineteeth- and twentieth-century ceramics, glass and furniture. Just have a wander around – you'll be sure to find something you love.

—

35 Cinque Ports Street, TN31 7AD.
01797 226379

❖ GREAT DIXTER

Renowned gardener Christopher Lloyd built on the work of Edwin Lutyens, who designed both home and garden in 1910, to create one of Britain's most magnificent open houses. If you're travelling by car, you've no excuse – pop in to admire some truly extraordinary work, including arresting floral displays and an interior dotted with mid-century modern furniture commissioned by Lloyd himself.

—

Northiam, Rye, TN31 6PH.
01797 252878
www.greatdixter.co.uk

❖ THE SPIKE MILLIGAN CIRCULAR WALK FROM RYE TO WINCHELSEA

The comedian lived his last few years in Rye and is buried in nearby Winchelsea's St Thomas's Church – this three-mile marsh walk between the two is terrific. Key sites along the way include Camber Castle, the Royal Military Canal and The New Inn pub, which makes a top stop for lunch.

—

www.dunescape.co.uk/things-to-do/spike-milligan-circular-walk-from-rye-to-winchelsea/

❖ CAMBER SANDS

Four miles from Rye are the breathtaking Camber Sands, a sprawl of undulating dunes bordered by marram grasses and sweet chestnut fences that stop the sands shifting from the broad beach. The Kit Kat Café is a great post from which to watch the kitesurfers, horseriders and sandcastle-builders at the water's edge. The number 100 and 101 buses run from the centre of Rye to the village of Camber, taking just fifteen minutes. From there, it's just a two-minute walk to the beach.

LEWES

It might seem quite contrary to head to the South Coast and miss the sea, but then Lewes is a rather contrary town. Indeed its sense of independence is so strong that in 2008 it even invented its own currency, the Lewes Pound. Little of this anarchic nature is overtly on display though in a town notable for its pleasing aspect. Handsome Regency buildings on Albion Street give way to the sweet little shops and shiplapped old cottages of Cliffe High Street, as well as the pretty Keere street further down. There are other less obvious pleasures to be discovered too. Like Pell's Pool (Brook Street), a carefully preserved 47-metre long Victorian lido surrounded by trees and a lawn, and the arresting ruins of Lewes Priory Park (Cockshut Road). Or the impressive medieval St Michael's Church (158 High Street), which was decorated with murals by Bloomsbury Group locals Vanessa Bell and Duncan Grant. A walk to their stunning house and walled garden, Charleston, six miles away, is a terrific way to experience the beauty of the South Downs. Other local walks include strolls along the River Ouse to the picturesque village of Barcombe and a clamber through the town's alleyways up to the imposing eleventh-century ruins of the motte-and-bailey Lewes Castle. If you're here on Bonfire Night, it's a fantastic perch from which to watch the Bonfire Society's famous – and famously raucous – Grand Union Procession. But to really appreciate the unique appeal of this little town you're far better off coming when the crowds are elsewhere.

—

Get there: *Trains run direct from London Victoria and London Bridge, taking around one hour.*

♣ CHARLESTON

In 1916, Vanessa Bell and Duncan Grant turned this elegant manor house into the country home of the Bloomsbury Group, remodelling its interiors with décor that would draw on everything from Italian frescoes to the contemporary work of the post-Impressionists. Its walls are also adorned with pieces by Renoir, Picasso, Derain, Sickert, and Delacroix... and the gardens are equally stunning.

—

Firle, BN8 6LL.
01323 811265
www.charleston.org.uk

❖ HARVEY'S BREWERY

On the eastern bank of the River Ouse, this imposing Victorian brewery features a shop selling more than 20 types of own-brewed ale – including an eye-watering eight per cent Christmas Ale and many other seasonal tipples using hops from Sussex, Kent and Surrey. Sample them at the adjacent John Harvey Tavern or at the town's two best pubs, The Gardener's Arms (46 High Cliffe Street) and The Lewes Arms (1 Mount Place).

—

The Bridge Wharf Brewery, 6 Cliffe High Street, BN7 2AH.
01273 480217
www.harveys.org.uk

❖ THE TOM PAINE PRINTING PRESS & PRESS GALLERY

Named for seventeenth-century revolutionary Thomas Paine, who lived opposite at Bull House for six years and whose portrait graces the Lewes Pound, this fascinating shop and gallery displays and sells a wide range of printed ephemera in a space replicating an eighteenth-century wooden press. There are regular demonstrations (which you can book ahead), but it's fun just browsing.

—

151 High Street, BN7 1XU.
01273 476265
www.tompaineprintingpress.com

❖ ANNE OF CLEVES HOUSE

Set in a medieval timber house bequeathed to
Henry VIII's fourth wife, this little museum has
not only history, but also a fantastic location in
the pretty area of Southover. Its garden, complete
with traditional Tudor planting schemes, is also a
captivating spot in which to take tea and pretend
you've slipped back a few centuries in time.

—

52 Southover High Street, BN7 1JA.

01273 474610

www.sussexpast.co.uk/properties-to-discover/anne-of-cleves-house

✤ SOUTHOVER GRANGE GARDENS

Just a five-minute walk away from the Anne of Cleves House, these sixteenth-century walled gardens are wonderful. Essentially two gardens split by the gurgling Winterbourne stream, they include magnificent trees and a wildflower area. The Tea Hatch also serves excellent tea and cake.

Southover House, Southover Road, BN7 1AB.

01273 484999

www.lewes.gov.uk

RHS WISLEY

It's hard to describe how unusual RHS Wisley is in terms of its horticultural appeal. It's not a park or a formal garden, or the kind of estate favoured by centuries of landed gentry, but a series of contrasting gardens spread out over 60 acres – the size of 34 football pitches. The different spaces and their juxtaposition will engage all your senses and are sure to have budding horticulturalists and garden enthusiasts hooked for hours. The famous six-metre-wide Mixed Borders, running 128 metres (420 feet) long, are the star players in terms of colour and drama, but all the gardens are meticulously designed to keep interest throughout the year and throughout each section. The famous rhododendrons and azaleas that set Battleston Hill alight each spring are just one feature of the woodland garden, followed by the hot, sumptuous colours of the Rose Borders in summer and the scrumping opportunities offered in the Fruit Field come autumn. Even in the depths of winter, Wisley is worth a wander to catch snowdrops peeking out with the promise of new life. And just around the corner is the Norman village of Ripley, which makes a trip down to this neck of the woods even sweeter. A four-mile walk from the garden along the banks of the River Wey (see page 77), it's home to the Michelin-starred restaurant Drake's (see page 75) – a just reward after an immersive morning at one of Surrey's most enjoyable day-trip destinations.

———

Wisley Lane, Woking, Surrey, GU23 6QB.
0845 260 9000, www.rhs.org.uk/gardens/wisley

Get there: *Trains run from London Waterloo to West Byfleet (two miles away) and Woking (four miles away), taking around half an hour. On summer weekdays a bus service runs to the garden from both.*

✤ THE GLASSHOUSE & GLASSHOUSE LAKE

Three different climatic zones are housed within this cathedral-like glasshouse and together they encompass alien-looking desert plants, huge cacti, exotic orchids and towering tree ferns. The Glasshouse itself also overlooks an adjoining semi-circular lake. For fantastic views of both, and to fully appreciate the work of its designer Tom Stuart-Smith, climb the hill to Fruit Mount.

—

RHS Wisley, Wisley Lane, Woking, GU23 6QB.
0845 260 9000
www.rhs.org.uk/gardens/wisley/garden-highlights/the-glasshouse

❖ THE ANCHOR

This riverside pub makes a pleasing walk from Wisley, just one-and-a-half miles away from the garden's entrance. And once there, supping a pint at one of the canalside tables in the huge garden watching the barges roll by is a real treat. As is its fetching interior and traditional pub grub.

—

Pyrford Lock, Wisley, Woking, GU23 6QW.
01932 342507
www.anchorpyrford.co.uk

❖ DRAKE'S

Drake's has won a Michelin star for twelve consecutive years and it's easy to see why. Chef Steve Drake's modern, British-focused cuisine marries substance and style with aplomb. Dishes are served in an easy-going and airy garden-facing room of an elegant Georgian building.

—

The Clock House, High Street, Ripley, GU23 6AQ.
01483 224777
www.drakesrestaurant.co.uk

✤ RIPLEY NURSERIES & FARM SHOP

Founder Arthur Luff's nursery has been going strong for more than 100 years, with various expansions creating an excellent shop for gardeners and foodies alike. If you're in a car, you'll be tempted to fill your boot from the huge array of plants, but leave space for Fatherson Bakery cakes and cheeses from the High Weald Dairy.

—

Portsmouth Road, Ripley, GU23 6EY.
01483 225090
www.ripleynurseries.co.uk

❖ RIPLEY TO PYRFORD LOCK WALK

To enjoy a small section of the 20-mile Wey Navigation, take the easy three-mile waterside walk from Ripley to Pyrford Lock. En route you'll pass a curious-looking brick tower known as John Donne's tower, which bears a blue plaque declaring that 'John Donne, Poet and Dean of St Pauls, lived here 1600–1604'. It's unlikely that he did, but he did live at nearby Pyrford Lock.

www.fancyfreewalks.org/Surrey

HENLEY-ON-THAMES

For five days each July, Henley-on-Thames is filled to bursting with thousands of Pimm's-drinking rowing fans in striped blazers who descend on the town for the annual Henley Royal Regatta, the rowing tournament that has been held here since 1839. But for the rest of the year, this medieval market town is a quiet, sleepy settlement on the banks of the Thames that makes a fine starting point for some scenic walks on the southern Chiltern Hills. The walks range in length, from a particularly appealing three miles along the Hamble Valley from Henley to Hambleton, to a nine-mile circular stroll through rolling hills to the stately home of Stonor Park. The National Trust's Grey's Court, a Tudor building with a beautiful walled garden, also makes for a great excursion just over two miles out of town. Whichever walk you decide to take will involve mixed woodland and green fields set in gently rolling valleys, and to have Henley at the start and finish is a real bonus. Oxford's oldest settlement, reputedly founded in Roman times, is an absorbing mix of art galleries, antique shops, pubs and cafés set in listed buildings – some 300 of them – dating as far as the fourteenth century.

—

Get there: *Trains run direct from London Paddington, taking around one hour.*

❖ THE ANGEL ON THE BRIDGE

A proper old-school alehouse in an eighteenth-century beamed building – pubs rarely come better than this, especially if the sun is shining and you've bagged a seat on the riverside terrace (or you've arrived by boat to use the pub's own mooring). The interior is welcoming too, particularly on a cold winter's evening next to the roaring log fire with a pint of local Brakspear ale in your hand.

—

Thameside, RG9 1BH.
01491 410678
www.theangelhenley.com

❖ THE BOHUN GALLERY

This small but well-curated space specialises in contemporary British fine art and the work of surrealist artist and printmaker Julian Trevelyan, who produced much of his work in Paris in the company of artistic greats Max Ernst, Joan Miro and Picasso. His fascinating pieces are accompanied by regularly rotating solo exhibitions alongside occasional sculpture work in the garden.

15 Reading Road, RG9 1AB.
01491 576228
www.bohungallery.co.uk

❖ HOTEL DU VIN & BISTRO

As with every branch of Hotel du Vin, this one, housed in a series of former brewery buildings, is filled with character and atmosphere. Its light central courtyard is the perfect place for lunch and the whitewashed brick and wooden floored bistro is filled with period furnishings. But it's the food that's the star – modern European dishes done simply but with real skill.

New Street, RG9 2BP.
0844 736 4258
www.hotelduvin.com/locations/henley-on-thames

❖ GORVETT & STONE

In a quaint little shop on the high street, Gorvett & Stone sells a wondrous range of chocolate treats. Its signature is the chocolate 'fish and chips': a Valrhona milk chocolate fish in a little bucket with white chocolate 'chips'. Other temptations include bags of chocolate honeycomb made from honey produced by local bees and 'exploding' chocolate frogs filled with popping candy.

21 Duke Street, RG9 1UR.

01491 414485

www.gorvettandstone.com

❖ RIVER & ROWING MUSEUM

Even if you've no interest in the sport, the River
& Rowing Museum is an enjoyable and absorbing
space. Exhibits cover not only rowing, but also
nearby rivers, the history of the town and, for
younger visitors, local author Kenneth Grahame's
The Wind in the Willows. 3D models, music and
lighting are used to bring the magical story
(and national treasure) to life.

Mill Meadows, RG9 1BF.
01491 415600
www.rrm.co.uk

GASTRONOMY & LUXURY

WHITSTABLE

The South-East is stuffed with top seafood destinations, but winsome Whitstable with its hillocks of glistening oyster shells is a real gourmand's paradise. It began back in 1856 when fisherman Richard 'Leggy' Wheeler's wife Mary Ann opened Wheeler's Oyster Bar (8 High Street) as a tiny parlour serving the town's famous native oysters to sixteen lucky diners. It continues today with The Whitstable Oyster Fishery Company (Horsebridge Road), The Crab and Winkle (South Quay) and all manner of first-class food and drink outlets on the picturesque High Street and Harbour Street. Along the former lie the rustic Samphire bistro (4 High Street), which serves local fish, meat and seasonal produce, the alluring Tea & Times (36A High Street), a tea-house-cum-newsstand with amazing cakes, and the marvellous Offy (5 High Street), the perfect place to pick up some Kent ale or wine to accompany your meal at Wheeler's (where you can bring your own) across the road. On adjoining Harbour Street, Elliott's @ No.1 Harbour Street has a regularly changing menu and a good ambience from morning to night, and the David Brown Delicatessen (28A Harbour Street) serves top-notch, tapas-style goodies. And finally, the late-medieval Tudor Tea Rooms (29 Harbour Street) might seat you at the table where local celebrity Peter Cushing fittingly dined regularly. Get here early, with an empty stomach, stay late, taking in as much as you can, and you still won't have sampled all the gastronomic delights of Whitstable.

—

Get there: *Trains run direct from London Victoria and London St Pancras International, taking around 90 minutes.*

❧ WHITSTABLE CASTLE & GARDENS

A short walk from the seafront, the gardens of this fairytale castle are a wonderful place in which to enjoy a snack al fresco. Try a gourmet meze selection from JoJo's (2 Herne Bay Road), or choose from the castle's own delectable range of cakes and nibbles in its tea rooms, which provide a sneak peek into the castle's mock-Tudor interior.

—

Tower Hill, CT5 2BW.

01227 281726

www.whitstablecastle.co.uk/the-castle

❧ THE OLD NEPTUNE

Pictures of an alluring alehouse in Whitstable can almost certainly be identified as the beachside Old Neptune, a charming establishment that looks out to sea and the Isle of Sheppey. If it's full, the seaside shack The Forge (in the Fisherman's Huts, Sea Wall) has deck chairs, wine and local beer, as well as oysters, doughnuts and ice cream.

—

Marine Terrace, Island Wall, CT5 1EJ.

01227 272262

www.neppy.co.uk

♣ THE STREET

The best strip on Whitstable's coast is undoubtedly this 750-metre long spit of shingle that emerges from the Tankerton Slopes at low tide. Walk its length and turn back to enjoy the scene of the groyne-dotted coastline and its colourful clapboard beach huts. Stick around until sunset for even more beautiful views.

—

Tankerton Beach, CT5 2BD.

❧ SUNDAE SUNDAE

Tiny Sundae Sundae's homemade ice creams, which include daily specials (mega-tasty salted caramel on a chocolate-and-nut dipped cone has been known to feature), draw long queues, but the interior of the shop is filled with such desirable sweets (egg and bacon flavour rock, anyone?) and retro knick-knacks that the waiting time will whizz by.

---

62 Harbour Street, CT5 1AG.

www.sundaesundae.co.uk/shop.html

❖ THE SPORTSMAN

Set on the old coast road between Whitstable and
Faversham with the sea in front of it, salt marshes
behind it and a rustic, warm ambience inside, the
Michelin-starred Sportsman is an idyllic seaside
pub. It has not one but two fabulous tasting
menus, including a modest five course one at just
£45 per person.

—

Faversham Road, Seasalter, CT5 4BP.
01227 273370
www.thesportsmanseasalter.co.uk

BAILIFFSCOURT HOTEL & SPA

Bailiffscourt Hotel and Spa is that rare thing: a luxury getaway just minutes away from a beautiful stretch of South Downs coast. Climping Beach, an open expanse of pebbles and sand dotted with sculpture-like wooden groynes, is only a few hundred yards away from the hotel and its 30 acres of private parkland. It's the perfect place to run, walk or simply sit and watch the kitesurfers wrestle with the wild waves. Mind you, it could be tough to tear yourself away from the captivating collection of mock-Tudor buildings (pictured left) that make up the hotel and spa, and that's before you indulge in the treatments on offer. These include day packages with the usual facials and manicures, as well as massages and themed signature treatments; the 90-minute Mediterranean Float is a luxurious all-over face and body treatment that uses aromatherapy balm to summon scents from the Med, and A Brush with Heaven uses a variety of brushes in all sizes and textures to relax and smooth your skin. But to really benefit from the idyllic location and atmosphere, an overnight stay is the way to go. As night falls, the Bailiffscourt becomes ablaze with soft, warm light that gives it a magical feel, which is further heightened by the candlelit restaurant inside and the peacocks wandering in the gardens beyond. But best of all, you get to enjoy all the spa facilities (including indoor and outdoor pools), as well as the nearby activities on the following pages.

Climping Street, Climping, West Sussex, BN17 5RW.
01903 723511, www.hshotels.co.uk/bailiffscourt-hotel-and-spa

Get there: *Trains run from London Bridge and London Victoria to Littlehampton, three miles away, taking just over 90 minutes. From there, a five-minute taxi ride will take you to the hotel.*

❖ CLIMPING TO WEST BEACH WALK

Just five minutes from Bailiffscourt is Climping Beach, and a half an hour walk from there brings you to West Beach. You'll get views of the South Downs to the north and Littlehampton seaside resort and the River Arun to the east. En route, the West Beach Nature Reserve might yield a shark's egg case or fossil, and the West Beach Café (Rope Walk, Littlehampton) serves homemade ice cream and fish dishes, all in stunning settings courtesy of award-winning architect Asif Kahn.

❖ THE BLACK HORSE INN

There are few seaside pubs better-looking than The Black Horse, an eighteenth-century smugglers' inn. Nowadays, the bar and restaurant are filled with more genteel folk enjoying huge portions of good pub food and a strong selection of real ales. The beer garden and decking area are excellent in the summer and it's just a five-minute walk from Climping Beach.

—

Climping Street, Littlehampton, BN17 5RL.
01903 715175

❖ LITTLEHAMPTON

The ramshackle charm of Littlehampton has drawn in a mixed crowd of visitors in its time, albeit not quite of the same calibre as revered historical figures like Byron and Constable. But with its impressive contemporary architecture, plenty of eateries, interesting shops and old-school Harbour Park fairground, there's a lot working in its favour. The gorgeous East and West beaches, nice and quiet out of peak season, make it a sure-fire winner.

❖ WAY OUT THERE & BACK

This long-established arts, crafts and new-age shop and gallery is worth a poke around for contemporary artworks by locals as well as a wide range of incense and essential oils. The Special Little Things Artisan Market, held on the last Saturday of each month in the same courtyard, is also one to catch.

—

2 Evans Garden, Arcade Road, Littlehampton, BN17 5AP.
01903 722666
www.loca.org.uk/index2.html

❖ EAST BEACH CAFÉ

Built years before his world-famous 2012 Olympic torch, Thomas Heatherwick's organic East Beach Café dominates the mile-long East Beach like a vast piece of driftwood. But it's the food that truly impresses; classic seaside fare includes locally caught fish and chips, burgers and the café's signature dish, salt and pepper squid.

—

Sea Road, Littlehampton, BN17 5NZ.
01903 731903
www.eastbeachcafe.co.uk

GOODWOOD

Quirky festivals, fast cars and horse-racing are three of Britain's favourite pastimes, and the trio come together in charming fashion at Goodwood, a country estate set in 12,000 acres of rolling Sussex Downs. It all began (as tales of old aristocracy so often do) with Wooster-like weekends in the 1930s in which family chums would pitch up to sample the country air and enjoy country pursuits such as racing cars along a long and winding front drive. This wheeze has since grown to comprise two annual weekend events that showcase the world's most amazing supercars and the world's most talented drivers at the early-summer Festival of Speed and the early-autumn Goodwood Revival. Both attract hundreds of thousands of spectators with classic cars spanning more than a century and the Revival featuring a dazzling display of period costumes. If you're not into cars but are into dressing up and star-spotting, Goodwood also hosts a summer of horseracing events culminating in the Glorious Goodwood Festival – a spectacle that attracts debs and celebs in equal measure to have a flutter on the horses that race around the 200-year-old course. And it's all held in the opulent environs of an estate that houses a hotel, two pay-and-play golf courses, a number of fine restaurants and the Cass Sculpture Park, in which more than 80 changing sculptures create an ever-evolving landscape of harmonious or contrasting forms throughout the year.

—

The Goodwood Estate, Chichester, West Sussex, PO18 0PX.
01243 755055, www.goodwood.com

Get there: *Trains run from London Victoria to Chichester, four miles away, taking around 90 minutes. From there, a ten-minute taxi ride will take you to the Goodwood Estate.*

❖ CHICHESTER

This impressive ancient town, just three miles from Goodwood, has enough history to keep fans absorbed for days, but it also packs a cultural punch. Standouts include a terrific collection of twentieth-century British art at Pallant House Gallery (9 North Pallant) and works by Marc Chagall, Graham Sutherland and John Piper at Chichester Cathedral (West Street). There's also Chichester Festival Theatre (Oaklands Park), an artistic powerhouse with award-winning shows.

❖ THE FOX GOES FREE

Londoners fed up with real foxes might not take to the name, but there's no doubting the appeal of this beautiful countryside pub. Its huge garden and sprawling flint and stone building draw you into an oak-beamed interior that's just as impressive as the views across to Levin and the North Downs.

—

Charlton Road, Chichester, PO18 0HU.

01243 811461

www.thefoxgoesfree.com

❖ FIELD & FORK

The clean, white brickwork and bright conservatory of this Chichester stalwart are the ideal setting for its refined cuisine. Le Gavroche-trained chef patron Sam Mahoney sources seasonal local produce to create delectable modern Mediterranean dishes. A three-course set menu is available for a very reasonable £22.95.

—

4 Guildhall Street, Chichester, PO19 1NJ.
01243 789915
www.fieldandfork.co.uk

❖ PARK HOUSE HOTEL & SPA

The croquet lawn, tennis courts, boot room and outdoor pool say it all – this is sheer indulgence. But it's set in the kind of understated country house which replaces airs and graces with a friendly, hospitable attitude and charming staff. Spa packages range from half-day and evening to full-day and mini-breaks.

Bepton, near Midhurst, GU29 0JB.
01730 819000
www.parkhousehotel.com

❖ MIDHURST

Come summer, the polo set descend on this chocolate-box Sussex Weald town to watch teams fight it out for the Gold Cup at Cowdray Park, where the ruins of the Tudor manor house (pictured above) make an atmospheric backdrop. The rest of the time it's a slice of rural England at its best, with lots of independent shops on North Street to browse. Just eight miles north of Goodwood, it's only half an hour in a taxi across the picture perfect South Downs National Park.

MERSEA ISLAND

Nine miles south-east of Colchester lies England's most easterly island. Or at least part-time island… Connected to Essex by an ancient Roman causeway known as the Strood, Mersea Island is regularly cut off from the mainland when the causeway is submerged by the rising tide. It makes getting here a real adventure, but once you're safely across it's a serene and peaceful destination. Some marvellous walks along the salt marshes trace the steps of rhinos, Romans and smugglers, and oyster beds are quietly lapped by the gentle waters of a salt creek. If you're lucky, you might discover a fossil on the beaches and cliffs of East Mersea, where shark's teeth and monkey, bear and bison bones dating back 300,000 years have been found. But even the unlucky will have no trouble finding the superb Gigas 'rocks' and Colchester Native Oysters harvested from the many beds along the coast and declared by Pliny the Elder more than 2,000 years ago to be 'the only good thing to come out of Britain'. There are very specific reasons for the oysters' superior flavour, not least the clean, plankton-rich creek waters they mature in, but the proof of the pudding of course lies in the eating. Luckily, this is easily done at eateries such as The Company Shed (pictured left), the West Mersea Oyster Bar (Coast Road) and East Mersea's Mehalah's at Oysters & Ale (East Mersea Road), where you can also pick up a picnic hamper.

—

Get there: *Frequent trains run from London Liverpool Street to Colchester, ten miles away, taking around one hour. From there, the number 67B bus runs to West Mersea.*

❖ MERSEA VINEYARD & BREWERY

Take a tour of the vineyard on this 10-acre site in East Mersea and sample both the wine and beer before stocking up on your favourites in the courtyard café. The beers make particularly good gifts, with colourful labels and equally colourful names – anyone for Mersea Mud?

—

Rewsalls Lane, East Mersea, CO5 8SX.
01206 385900
www.vineyard.merseabrewery.co.uk

❖ THE ARTCAFÉ

Part café, part gallery, this homely space in the heart of West Mersea is run by husband and wife James and Maggie Weaver who, together with their daughter, make most of the food here. They do classic fry-ups and delicious cakes, and recently added the Cake-Hole deli next door.

—

2 Coast Road, West Mersea, CO5 8QE.
01206 385234
www.islandartcafe.co.uk

❧ THE COMPANY SHED

Mersea's most famous restaurant is this
unprepossessing shack on the beach that's been
serving Colchester Natives for decades. Unusually,
you can bring your own bread as well as booze
here; a bottle of dry white Mehalah from the
Mersea Vineyard & Brewery will make the perfect
accompaniment to your superfresh seafood.

—

129 Coast Road, West Mersea, CO5 8PA.
01206 382700
www.thecompanyshed.co

❧ CUDMORE GROVE COUNTRY PARK

This nature reserve and country park is made up of grassland, forest and meadows, and all are home to an abundance of wildlife. There's also a sandy beach that looks across the Colne estuary to Brightlingsea, as well as lots of enjoyable manmade oddities to enjoy on the various walks and trails – look out for the Second World War pillboxes and the remains of a sixteenth-century blockhouse fort.

Bromans Lane, East Mersea, CO5 8UE.
01206 383868
www.visitparks.co.uk/places/cudmore-grove

❧ LADY GRACE BOAT TRIPS

Hop aboard Stacey's 21-foot open launch for a 20-minute, £3 sightseeing trip around Packing Shed Island (pictured above), where oysters used to be packed as far back as the 1850s, and where the remains of the old oyster beds are still visible. Alternative themed trips cater for kids, and wildlife and birdwatching trips are available come winter. If you're staying the night, opt for the slightly longer sunset cruise.

West Mersea Jetty.
07791 859624
www.essexboattrips.co.uk

COWORTH PARK

Perched on the borders of Windsor Great Park, Coworth Park Country Spa is a typically enchanting yet refreshingly modern luxury destination. The idyll begins with a vast and stunning wildflower meadow whose colourful cornflowers, poppies and buttercups shine against the wedding-cake-white of the Georgian mansion that sits behind it (pictured left). Set in 245 acres of countryside comprising two polo fields, tennis courts, an equestrian centre and a delicate rose garden, the hotel is indeed pure opulence. But unless you plan to stay, the focus of your visit will be the semi-underground grass-roofed building protruding from a man-made hill: the spa. Just a couple of minutes' walk from the house, this innovation in architecture awards visitors with a soothing sense of quiet and privacy, discreetly shielding the eight treatment rooms, gym, heated pool and Spatisserie from prying eyes; a boon if you're one of the many celebs who comes here to unwind among the tasteful art and sculptures. You can join them for a relatively modest sum – spa days including a two-course lunch start at £150.

—

Coworth Park, Blacknest Road, Ascot, Berkshire, SL5 7SE.
01344 876 600, www.dorchestercollection.com/en/ascot/coworth-park

Get there: *Trains run from London Waterloo to Ascot, three miles away, taking around one hour. From there, a ten-minute taxi ride will take you to the spa.*

❖ WINDSOR GREAT PARK & CASTLE

Across Virginia Water (see page 114) and a two-mile walk from Coworth Park is Windsor Great Park, once part of a vast Norman hunting forest enclosed in the late thirteenth century. It now covers over 2,000 hectares of land incorporating a deer park, gardens and woodland – a six-mile ramble from the spa leads you neatly to the gates of Windsor Castle.

—

SL4 2HT.
01753 860222
www.theroyallandscape.co.uk

❖ BRAY

For a very special occasion, lunch or dine in the nearby parish of Bray, home to no less than three Michelin-starred restaurants. Be sure to book well in advance for a table at Alain Roux's three-star Waterside Inn (Ferry Road) or Heston Blumenthal's three-star Fat Duck (High Street, picture above), or for shorter-notice bookings try Heston's second offering, The Hind's Head (High Street). Three spectacular establishments in equally spectacular settings.

❖ ASCOT RACECOURSE

Ascot racecourse is home to the country's most famous horse racing meeting, Royal Ascot, which attracts approximately 300,000 visitors over five days of racing. But don't worry about packing a fancy hat – outside of Royal Ascot season there's no formal dress code in the grandstand and an annual calendar of events includes outdoor film screenings and air displays.

—

Ascot, SL5 7JX.
www.ascot.co.uk

❧ VIRGINIA WATER

Set on the southern edge of Windsor Great Park (see page 112), this lake is bordered by some decidedly unusual features, including a 100-foot-high totem pole and part of a ruined city imported from North Africa. A lakeside walk of around four and a half miles takes you past these as well as numerous picturesque picnic spots.

114

✤ THE THATCHED TAVERN

Two miles from both Ascot Racecourse and
Coworth Park, this wood-beamed seventeenth-
century inn is an excellent station for a pint of
local ale on a sunny terrace. In keeping with its
upper-crust location it also serves a terrific range
of wines and champagne by the glass.

—

Cheapside, Ascot, SL5 7QG.
01344 620874
www.thethatchedtavern.co.uk

OXFORD

The city of dreaming spires has been attracting students and visitors to its colleges since the Middle Ages, and if it's your first visit, a tour of the college buildings should sit at the top of your list. The fourteenth-century Christ Church College is home to the hallowed cloisters of Oxford Cathedral, while Keble College is a must for its intricate brickwork by William Butterfield as well as Holman Hunt's painting, *Light of the World*. But Oxford also has much to enjoy beyond the architecture and art of its colleges and museums, thanks in part to its location at the junction of the Thames and Cherwell rivers. A relaxing riverside walk or punt from Magdalen bridge along the Cherwell will take you up to The Victoria Arms pub in Old Marston (Mill Lane), or you could hire a bike and head to the nearby Port Meadow, which is listed in the Domesday book. A potter around Oxford's interesting shops also makes for a rewarding day trip – Truck Store (101 Cowley Road), for example, sells CDs, vinyls and books, and hosts regular live music performances. And the nineteenth-century Pitt Rivers Museum (accessed through the Museum of Natural History, Parks Road) is a first-class attraction that hosts temporary exhibitions alongside permanent collections of archaeological and ethnographic objects, including the ever-fascinating shrunken heads of ancient South America. To cap it all, the city's gastronomic offerings are plentiful, with restaurants and cafés to serve all tastes. But for Oxford's best gastronomic experience you'll need to head to nearby Great Milton and Raymond Blanc's Le Manoir aux Quat'Saisons (see overleaf).

—

Get there: *Trains run direct from London Paddington, taking around one hour.*

❧ LE MANOIR AUX QUAT'SAISONS

At the dreamy Great Milton Manor, Raymond Blanc has created a rural idyll just half an hour's drive from the centre of Oxford. It's a treat of an old-school country house hotel set in 30 acres of grounds incorporating a herb garden, vegetable garden and mushroom garden. But it's the food in the two-Michelin star restaurant that's the real luxury here. Order the five- or seven-course tasting menu to experience the best of it.

—

Church Road, Great Milton, OX44 7PD.
01844 278881
www.belmond.com/ le-manoir-aux-quat-
saisons-oxfordshire

✣ ASHMOLEAN DINING ROOM

Sitting above the Palladian splendour of Oxford's
Ashmolean Museum, the light and airy rooftop of
the Ashmolean Dining Room is a fitting venue for
modern European meals served on pale oak tables.
Sliding glass doors ensure a seamless transition
from interior to exterior, making it a pleasure to
eat here whether inside or out.

Beaumont Street, OX1 2PH.
01865 610406
www.benugo.com/restaurants/ashmolean-dining-room

❖ OXFORD UNIVERSITY BOTANIC GARDEN

Britain's oldest botanic garden has approximately 5,000 different plant species packed into its two hectares, which include a fernery, seven glasshouses and a walled garden. And just outside Oxford, the garden's Harcourt Arboretum (Oxford Lodge, Peacock Gate) has one of the best collection of trees in the county, with some of the oldest redwoods in the UK.

—

Rose Lane, OX1 4AZ.
01865 286690
www.botanic-garden.ox.ac.uk

❖ OXFORD COVERED MARKET

More than 200 years old and still going strong, this market sells a broad range of produce along four long avenues. Visit the likes of the Alpha Bar, Oxford Cheese Company, David John Butchers and Nash's Bakery to put together a hamper to take to the Botanic Garden (see opposite), which is just a ten-minute walk away. An ideal place to take shelter should the weather turn.

—

Market St, OX1 3DZ.
www.oxford-coveredmarket.co.uk

❖ MAGDALEN ARMS

The duck-egg blue exterior is the first indication of this old-school tavern's transformation into an above-par gastropub. Whether you choose to eat outside on the wrap-around terrace or inside at a communal table, you'll eat well for a reasonable price. It's a fine drinking den too and there's a monthly flea market on the terrace.

—

243 Iffley Road, OX4 1SJ.
01865 243159
www.magdalenarms.co.uk

FAMILY FRIENDLY

CHISLEHURST CAVES

There is something magical about natural caves, but something altogether awe-inspiring about manmade caves. As illustrations of human ingenuity, determination and skill, they're always a thrill to explore. So Londoners are lucky to have Chislehurst so close. Dating back to the early thirteenth century, this 22-mile labyrinth of tunnels buried 30 metres below Kent woodlands makes a wonderful trip out of town whatever your age. But its spooky lamplit interior and fascinating history, vividly envoked by the occasional tableaux and informative guides, make it particularly good fun for kids. On a 45-minute tour you learn how the tunnels were originally dug out to provide the chalk needed in the production of bricks for the building of London, before becoming a munitions store in the First World War. In the 1930s they were used for mushroom growing and in the 1960s were transformed into a music venue – David Bowie and Jimi Hendrix were just two of the acclaimed acts that played here. But it was in the Second World War that the Chislehurst Caves came into their own, when they were turned into the largest underground air-raid shelter in the country. At the height of the Blitz, they housed over 15,000 people and contained a hospital and chapel, all lit by electricity. This little slice of London history is utterly absorbing, enormous fun and a godsend on a rainy holiday Monday.

———

Caveside Hill, Old Hill, Chislehurst, Kent, BR7 5NL.
020 8467 3264, www.chislehurst-caves.co.uk

Get there: *Trains run from London Charing Cross and London Cannon Street to Chislehurst, taking around half an hour. From there, it's a short walk to the caves.*

❖ PETTS WOOD AND HAWKWOOD

Managed by the National Trust, the 138 hectares here contain a working farm and ancient woodland that come together to create a natural playground for kids and a haven for all kinds of wildlife. Try to catch a demonstration of the ancient tradition of charcoal burning, carried out regularly as part of the site's woodland management.

—

Chislehurst, BR5 1NZ.
01732 810378
www.nationaltrust.org.uk/petts-wood-and-hawkwood

❖ FOOTS CRAY MEADOWS

The mixed woodland, riverbanks and grasslands of this luscious country park contain numerous walks and wildlife-spotting opportunities, but a gentle horse ride makes the most of the meadows. Book a private hack at the adjoining North Cray and Sidcup Riding School (25 Parsonage Lane) where there's also a large children's playground for the littler, non-riding folk.

—

North Cray Road, Sidcup, DA14 5AG.
www.footscraymeadows.org

❖ DOWN HOUSE

The former home of English naturalist Charles Darwin and his family is a total joy. Step into the study in which he wrote *On the Origin of Species* and wander through the gardens and greenhouse that inspired him during the 40 years he lived here. Learn of both his house and work in an absorbing exhibition before having tea and cake in the pretty tearoom or, if it's sunny, on the even prettier patio.

—

Luxted Road, Downe, BR6 7JT.
01689 859119
www.english-heritage.org.uk/visit/places/home-of-charles-darwin-down-house

❖ CHISLEHURST & SCADBURY PARK NATURE RESERVE

The little town of Chislehurst feels a world away from central London, which is actually only thirteen miles to the north. Woodlands, country lanes, a duck pond and grassy common, as well as the quaint Royal Parade, cute cottages and even cuter wildlife (particularly on Scadbury Park Nature Reserve) mean there is lots to enjoy on a local walk.

✤ THE RAMBLER'S REST

Facing a nice patch of rolling green park beyond the cricket ground, the cream clapboard-clad eighteenth-century Rambler's Rest couldn't be lovelier, with wood beams, a nice selection of real ales and hearty pub grub, plus a paved terrace with bench tables. Takeaway picnics for two start from £25.

5 Mill Place, Chislehurst, BR7 5ND.
020 8467 1734
www.ramblers.rest

ROCHESTER

Rolling into Rochester over the Medway is a great way to catch your first glimpse of this attractive town, with fine views of the Norman castle keep and the cathedral just visible above the rooftops. One of the best ways to explore it is to follow the trail of its most famous resident, Charles Dickens, via the informative leaflet from the Visitor Information Centre (95 High Street). This covers many of the town's key sites including: the seventeenth-century Guildhall (17 High Street); Rochester Cathedral, founded in 604 and the second oldest cathedral in the country; and the Vines (Crow Lane), formerly the priory vineyard of the cathedral. Further down High Street, you'll come across the newly refurbished Eastgate House and Dickens's Swiss Chalet where the author worked on some of his most famous novels. Along the way, Dickens-themed businesses like Sweet Expectations (87 High Street) and Dickens House Wine Emporium (53 High Street) cash in on the cachet, but it's the charity and antique shops that will delight shopaholics. Standouts are the Oxfam Shop (25–29 High Street), which features a 'music room and gentlemen's closet', and Baggins Book Bazaar (19 High Street), a bibliophile's treasure trove. Two miles away at Dickens World in Chatham, Dickens's documentation of the more seamy side of Victorian England can be enjoyed on a 90-minute tour, but exploring the real-world sites of so many of his books makes for an equally memorable experience for all ages.

—

Get there: *Trains run direct from Stratford International and London Bridge, taking between half an hour and one hour.*

❖ FIELDSTAFF ANTIQUES

This olde-worlde cornucopia of wonder sells everything from vintage clothing and haberdashery to tableware and ceramics. A little back room is filled with books and hundreds of postcard albums organised by theme and region, and upstairs you'll find a linen cupboard, as well as many more covetable bits and bobs in between. Hours of fun.

—

93 High Street, ME1 1LX.

01634 846144

www.fieldstaffantiques.com

❧ ROCHESTER CASTLE & CASTLE GARDENS

Kids will love the sense of danger as they wind up the worn stone spiral staircases of the twelfth-century keep, and the ice cream kiosk in the castle gardens will probably spur them on too. The latter make a top pitch for a picnic – buy supplies at The Deli (28 High Street) or the Garden House Café & Deli (98 High Street).

—

Castle Hill, ME1 1SW.

01634 335882

www.english-heritage.org.uk/visit/places/
rochester-castle/

❧ GUILDHALL MUSEUM

Housed in neighbouring Georgian and Victorian buildings, this absorbing museum should keep all ages happy for a while, with tiny ones enjoying simple interactive elements like steering a boat down the Medway. For older visitors, the gruesome Hulk Experience chillingly documents life for the prisoners incarcerated on converted old sailing ships on the Medway.

—

7 High Street, ME1 1PY.

01634 332680

✣ THE COOPERS ARMS

This late-medieval half-beamed inn is a slice of history as well as a great drinking den. The landlord can give you the lowdown on the resident ghost while you sup on one of Kent's locally-made beers and tuck into a classic roast.

—

10 St Margaret's Street, ME1 1TL.
01634 404298
www.thecoopersarms.co.uk

❖ THE DEAF CAT COFFEE BAR

This laidback, boho space serves rich coffee, yummy cakes, toasties and cold snacks. Just down the road, Bruno's Bakes and Coffee (10 High Street) is a worthy competitor for a light lunch. For more substantial fare, old-school café Tony Lorenzo (145 High Street) serves up pasties, while the upmarket modern British restaurant Topes (60 High Street) has a beautiful courtyard opposite the castle.

—

83 High Street, ME1 1LX.
07719 593960
www.thedeafcat.com

MARGATE

The regeneration of Kent's most famous seaside town has been the source of much debate among urban planners over the past decade, but it seems the wheels of Margate's arts-led revival – greased by the 2011 opening of the Turner Contemporary – are now firmly in motion. The economic neglect of recent times has left obvious scars, but the reopening of Dreamland (pictured left), an amusement park that dates back to the 1920s, appears to have galvanised the community and reestablished Margate as the day-trip destination du jour for retro fun and frolics. Every month sees new openings here, with seafood café/gallery Hantverk & Found (18 King Street) and shops like Haeckels (18 Cliff Terrace), which sells beauty products made from Margate seaweed, perhaps the most indicative of the town's reformed status. Most visitor sites are within easy walking distance of the train station, and a short stroll along the curved seafront brings you to the tiny Old Town where you'll find independent cafés, vintage shops and galleries. Head east beyond here and you'll reach Cliftonville with its derelict but photogenic art deco lido. But of course, for many, the main draw is still Margate's fabulous beach, known locally as The Sands. Buy some fish and chips from Peter's Fish Factory on The Parade and head down to devour them on the smart Harbour Steps. Hang about here until early evening and you may be treated to one of Margate's famous sunsets, just as spectacular now as in JMW Turner's day.

Get there: *Trains run direct from London Victoria and London Charing Cross, taking around two hours. High-speed trains from London St Pancras International take around 90 minutes.*

❖ TURNER CONTEMPORARY

Despite its clinical exterior, this David Chipperfield-designed building is totally enchanting inside, partly due to its huge two-storey window facing a mesmerising seascape. The gallery has played a key role in Margate's new-found popularity, hosting temporary exhibitions by the likes of Piet Mondrian, Grayson Perry and the gallery's namesake JMW Turner since opening in 2011.

Rendezvous, CT9 1HG.
01843 233000
www.turnercontemporary.org

✤ DREAMLAND

After being closed for a decade, the town's legendary amusement park is back with a cool, retro-themed design by Wayne Hemingway. The new park is opening in stages; 2015 saw the opening of key restored rides including the landmark Scenic Railway plus food stalls, arcades and a roller disco.

—

49–51 Marine Terrace, CT9 1XJ.
www.dreamland.co.uk

❖ BEBEACHED

This family-run restaurant and café on the atmospheric Harbour Arm marries home-style décor with excellent food. Service is always personable and the varied brunch, lunch and à la carte dishes make good use of local ingredients. The 'micropub' a couple of buildings along is a fine spot for pre- or post-grub drinks.

Margate Harbour Arm, CT9 1AP.
01843 226008
www.bebeached.co.uk

❖ THE SHELL GROTTO

This astonishing subterranean chamber has to be seen to be believed and the mystery surrounding how it came to be only adds to its allure. Was it an ancient temple? Or a room for a secret cult? We'll probably never know. But whoever was responsible sure put in the man hours – 4.6 million shells cover the grotto's walls forming breathtaking mosaics.

Grotto Hill, CT9 2BU.
01843 220008
www.shellgrotto.co.uk

❖ SCOTT'S FURNITURE MART

A vintage shopping haven set in an old ice-machine factory, Scott's is the cream of the crop when it comes to second-hand furniture and curios. A strong collection of mid-century items can also be found in the separate basement shop, Junk Deluxe. And for more mid-century homeware ingeniously coupled with blooming plants and flowers, ETC (35 Hawley Street) is a knockout.

—

The Old Iceworks, Bath Place, CT9 2BN.
01843 220653
www.scottsmargate.co.uk

HAMPTON COURT

Hampton Court may not seem like an obvious London 'escape', what with its proximity to the capital and the hundreds of tourists who descend on its grounds every day. Nevertheless, it's a top-notch family destination and the immediate vicinity offers a few alternative activities that will take you away from the crowds and into some peace and quiet (see overleaf). But first, that Palace, whose physical stature and grandeur are just the beginning. In the exploration of the origins of Thomas Wolsey's sumptuous palace complex, the additions by Henry VIII and the Wren-designed rebuild for William and Mary, it really comes to life. Though you'll need plenty of energy to do it justice. To give some sense of its scale, in August 1546 Henry hosted the French ambassador, his entourage of 200 and their staff plus 1,300 members of his own court for six days... Particular care is taken to engage younger visitors using play and games, costumed tours, presentations, a range of trails and the Magic Garden adventure playground, which is inspired by the palace's history. Older visitors shouldn't miss the Cumberland Art Gallery, whose collection includes works by Caravaggio, Holbein, Gainsborough and Canaletto. You can just visit the garden and the maze, but to miss out on a walk through the history that Hilary Mantel's *Wolf Hall* so thrillingly brought to life would be a real shame.

—

East Moseley, Surrey, KT8 9AU.
0844 482 7777, www.hrp.org.uk

Get there: *Trains run direct from London Waterloo, taking around 40 minutes.*

❖ HAMPTON COURT MAZE & GARDENS

The trapezoidal puzzle maze at Hampton Court is one of the most famous in the world and is fiendishly difficult to master, but huge fun nonetheless. If it's all too much like hard work, a stroll through the rest of the 60-acre gardens, including the Privy Gardens, should be much more relaxing. There is also plenty of wildlife to be found in the adjacent 750-acre Home Park.

—

East Moseley, KT8 9AU.
0844 482 7777
www.hrp.org.uk

❖ BOAT HIRE

Sit back and enjoy the views from one of Turks's charming riverboats, which ply the Thames between Hampton Court and Kingston. Or for your own quiet exploration, hire a day boat; Hampton Ferry Dayboats (Thames Street) lease adorable little blue and yellow four-seaters from £30 an hour.

—

Turks Boats, Turks Pier, Hampton Court, Barge Walk, East Molesey, KT8 9AS.
020 8546 2434
www.turks.co.uk

❖ RIVERSIDE WALKS

Hampton Court's riverside location makes a Thames Path walk an easy option on a day trip here, though managing all 30 miles of it to the Thames Barrier at Woolwich might be a tall order. But in less than an hour you can get to Kingston upon Thames and a surprisingly rural walk to Richmond takes only two hours.

❖ LE PETIT NANTAIS

A traditional French bistro may seem like an oddity here but it works wonderfully. The focus is on seafood and classic French dishes like steak tartare and fries, all served in a sunny, white space. Next door, the equally unexpected Lebanese restaurant Mezzet (43 Bridge Road) is hugely popular and just as elegant.

—

41 Bridge Road, East Moseley, KT8 9ER.
0208 979 2309
www.lepetitnantais.com

❧ THE ALBANY

Across the river from Hampton Court is the village of Thames Ditton. It's here you'll find The Albany, a modern and expansive riverside gastropub with enticing bar nibbles such as homemade sausage rolls and British seeded sprats. If you're in need of something more substantial after a day at the palace, they also serve full meals.

Queens Road, Thames Ditton, KT7 0QY.
0208 972 9163
www.the-albany.co.uk

WATERCRESS LINE

There are more than 200 steam railway lines in the UK and if they were ranked for popularity, there's a high chance the Mid-Hants Railway (otherwise known as the Watercress Line Steam Railway) would feature in the top ten. Chugging along the ten miles from Alresford to Alton, the polished Watercress Line's engines and spick-and-span carriages are just the beginning; it's what goes on behind the scenes that makes the line so special. Genial, good-natured staff and an imaginative range of themed events and activities are topped and tailed by the pretty Georgian towns of Alresford and Alton at either end of the line. At whichever point you begin your journey, once onboard you can sit back to take in the views, or liven things up by hopping on and off – at Ropley, for example, Harry Potter fans can walk in their hero's footsteps across the wrought-iron bridge once stationed in King's Cross, and gardeners can admire the imaginative topiary. Across the line from the station in Arlesford, an elevated picnic area is a handy post from which to snap other trains passing by. At Medstead & Four Marks station, the highest in southern England, there's the chance to stretch your legs on a lovely two-hour walk to Alton via the village of Chawton, taking in the home of Jane Austen. Steam trains, handsome Georgian towns, bags of history, Harry Potter and delightful topiary – what more could you ask of a family day out?

———

The Railway Station, Arlesford, Hampshire, SO24 9JG.
01962 733810, www.watercressline.co.uk

Get there: *Trains run direct from London Waterloo to Alton, taking just over one hour.*

✤ THE MILLENNIUM TRAIL & THE ALRE VALLEY TRAIL

Alresford's colourful Broad Street is filled with independent shops, cafés and pubs. It can be explored as part of the Millennium Trail, which is a scenic riverside walk to the River Alre that takes in the pretty thirteenth-century thatched Fulling Mill (pictured above), a fish farm and two duck ponds. It's a leisurely, mile-long circular walk dotted with illustated boards that give a great insight into the history and natural features of the village.

❖ ALLEN GALLERY

The small size of this gallery belies its impressive ceramics and pottery collection, which incorporates English, continental and oriental pottery, porcelain and tiles from 1250 to the present day. Next door, the Curtis Museum houses an eclectic and absorbing local history collection including Roman and Saxon artefacts.

—

10–12 Church Street, Alton, GU34 2BW.

01420 82802

www.hampshireculturaltrust.org.uk/allen-gallery

❖ THE GLOBE

Among the many pubs and coaching inns in Alresford, the seventeenth-century Globe stands out for its setting on the banks of the thirteenth-century Old Alresford Pond. Its selection of real ales on tap and delicious food only add to the charm – enjoy them after a walk round the lovely watercress meadows that give the railway line its name.

—

20 The Soke, Alresford, SO24 9DB.
01962 733118
www.theglobealresford.com

❖ JANE AUSTEN'S HOUSE MUSEUM

Numerous local walks lead past sites related to the eight years Jane Austen spent in the village of Chawton. The seventeenth-century cottage she lived in is the best one, featuring a range of artefacts in a setting that successfully evokes the author's time here. Bring a hamper of food and take it all in from the lovely garden.

—

Chawton, Alton, GU34 1SD.

01420 83262

www.jane-austens-house-museum.org.uk

❖ CARACOLI

The eighteenth-century exterior may look like an unlikely home for a decent cup of coffee, but with award-winning baristas, Caracoli is clearly the place caffeine-craving Londoners should head. Inside, an unexpectedly modern space sells handmade cakes and savoury dishes to eat in or take away. Enjoy in the courtyard garden or on one of the pavement tables outside.

—

15 Broad Street, Alresford, SO24 9AR.

01962 738730

www.caracoli.co.uk

GREAT MISSENDEN

Sometimes, the name and essence of a place can be perfectly in tune. And if Great Missenden were to conjure up notions of children's tales set in the countryside, it could not be more apt – this Buckinghamshire village was the home and workplace of author Roald Dahl for 36 years, until his death in 1990. The village has changed little in that time, its cobbled alleys and handsome high street still home to Gipsy House, Dahl's home, and many of the sites that inspired his stories, such as Crown House, the timber-framed building at 70 High Street that morphed into the 'norphanage' in *The BFG*. The addition in 2005 of the Roald Dahl Museum and Story Centre has made Great Missenden a very popular day trip for families, but the easy charm of the large village coupled with its setting in the pretty Misbourne river valley makes it hugely appealing to all ages. Even the train journey from Marylebone station through the rolling, sheep-filled fields of the Chiltern Hills is a delight. To discover it all at your leisure, pick up the Roald Dahl Village and Countryside Trail leaflet from the centre, or just strike out for a walk in the rolling countryside surrounding the village.

—

Get there: *Trains run direct from London Marylebone, taking around 45 minutes.*

❖ ROALD DAHL MUSEUM & STORY CENTRE

In an expansive space that's a joy for families to explore, Roald Dahl's fascinating story unfolds via imaginative galleries filled with accessible and entertaining panels, artefacts, photos and interactive elements. Look out for the author's extracted hip bone in his writing hut, the interior of which is the original from the garden of the Dahl family home.

—

81–83 High Street, HP16 0AL.
01494 892192
www.roalddahl.com

❖ ANGLING SPRING WOOD

This tangling ancient woodland, a short walk out of town, is home to the fallen 'Witching Tree' that inspired Roald Dahl's *Fantastic Mr Fox*. To get the most from it, download the two-hour talking tree trail, which corresponds with a map and ten carved posts in the woods and features the voices of actors such as Toby Jones.

—

www.chiltern.gov.uk/article/1983/
Angling-Spring-Woods

❖ ST PETER & ST PAUL CHURCH

This parish church is often frequented by children coming to pay homage to Roald Dahl, who is buried under a tree near some footprints of the BFG. But the interior has some interesting medieval touches for older fans, including a little carved head of past parish notables at the top of each nave pillar.

—

Church Lane, HP16 0BA.
01494 862352
www.missendenchurch.org.uk

❖ THE CROSS KEYS

Right in the heart of the village, this sixteenth-century coaching inn has everything you want from a village pub; it's dog- and child-friendly, features a nice garden outside and inglenook fireplaces inside and it does good food, from traditional sandwiches and pub classics to more adventurous fare in the restaurant. Homemade cakes too.

—

40 High Street, HP16 0AU.
01494 865373
www.crosskeysgreatmissenden.co.uk

✤ ALPHABET SOUP

Alphabet Soup has countless irresistable gifts that will make you want to spend, spend and spend. Luckily, their quirky collection of cyclist's lunchboxes and knitted monkey keyrings are sold at pocket-money prices, so you won't need to break the bank. Next door at Big Sky, sisters Kim White and Karen Sheehy also sell lots of stylish homeware, gifts and bits for the garden, and much of it is displayed in the courtyard outside.

---

69 High Street, HP16 0AL.
01494 868878
www.alphabetsoup.co.uk

COOL & QUIRKY

ASHWELL

London's commuter belt has many alluring villages, but few of them can list mummified rats in a mesmerising museum (see page 166), medieval graffiti (see St Mary's Church overleaf) and a hill fort (Arbury Banks) among their attributes. And few of them are as utterly charming as Hertfordshire's Ashwell, where human habitation can be traced back 4,000 years and where Ashwell Springs has been babbling away for more than a millennium. The architecture of this village is the real draw, paying tribute to its deep historical roots with gorgeous buildings spanning more than 500 years; High Street is home to the fourteenth- and fifteenth-century Forester Cottages while sweet sixteenth-century, timber-framed cottages can be found at the junctions of Rollys Lane and Mill Street. The seventeenth century then makes its mark on the imposing edifice of The Guild House (55 High Street), while the Victorian era comes to life in Ashwell Bury (11 Fordham Close), a house reconstructed by Edwin Lutyens in 1923 with a garden designed by famous landscaper Gertrude Jekyll. In among them, local shops tempt you in with homemade produce and locally grown fare, from honey by Ashwell beekeeper Stuart Greenbank sold at the wonderfully named Crumps butcher (3 Mill Street), to sausage rolls and cakes at Days of Ashwell (7 High Street), where all the baked goods are made on site. Packing up a lunch to enjoy on the spring's banks or in Swan Street's Ashwell Cottage Garden makes for a superb day in the country. Round it off with a visit to Rhubarb & Mustard (see page 165) for a souvenir piece of Ashwell pottery.

—

Get there: *Trains run direct from London King's Cross to Ashwell & Morden, taking around one hour.*

163

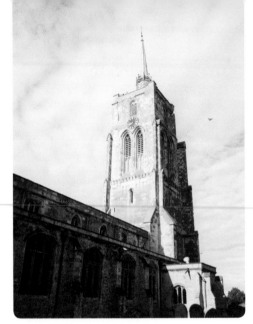

❖ ST MARY'S CHURCH

Despite some well-documented protestation from villagers regarding its noisy bells, the fourteenth-century St Mary's is a beauty of a village church, with a 176-foot spire and tower featuring medieval sketches of Old St Paul's and a softly lit interior in which original features span 300 years of craftsmanship. Perhaps most intriguing however is the early English and Latin graffiti that can be found carved into the base of the tower.

—

Mill Street, SG7 5QQ.
01462 742601
www.stmarysashwell.org.uk

❖ ROYSTON CAVE

This peculiar manmade cave shaped like a beehive is definitely worth the seven-mile trip from Ashwell. Believed to date back to medieval times, it features fantastic wall carvings depicting Christian scenes and saints, as well as some fainter, possibly older carvings interpreted by many as pagan symbols. Be sure to plan your visit in advance as the cave is only open on weekends and is closed from October to March.

—

Melbourn Street, Royston, SG8 7BZ.
01763 245484
www.roystoncave.co.uk

❖ RHUBARB & MUSTARD

Since it opened five years ago, this 'purveyor of fine things' has been constantly expanding its range of delicious morsels to eat and drink with the likes of Hertfordshire-made chocolates and local ice cream. Indulge youself with one of local baker Constance's homemade cakes at the coffee shop.

---

31 High Street, SG7 5NP.
01462 743462
www.rhubarbandmustard.co.uk

❖ BUSHEL & STRIKE

The pretty pastel Bushel & Strike has a fine range of cask ales from local brewer Charles Wells and a large, attractive garden in which to drink them. But this is a fantastic place to eat, and the restaurant prides itself on its modern European food, all served in cosy surrounds. One to book ahead for.

---

15 Mill Street, SG7 5LY.
01462 742394
www.bushelandstrike.co.uk

❖ ASHWELL VILLAGE MUSEUM

This two-storey gem, housed in a former Tudor shop, is stuffed with all manner of ephemera and craftsmanship spanning the village's history, including Roman jewellery, fragments of Tudor frescoes and a mummified black rat illustrating Hertfordshire's harsh struggle with The Plague in the 1300s. Heading towards its 80th birthday, it claims to be Britain's oldest village museum.

—

Swan Street, SG7 5NY.
01462 742956
www.ashwellmuseum.org.uk
NB: only open Sundays and Bank Holidays 2.30pm–5pm

SOUTHEND & AROUND

The stretch of Essex coast at the mouth of the River Thames has much to rival Kent and Sussex in the way of seaside destinations (see the following pages for highlights), and the jewel in its crown is the quintessentially British resort town of Southend-on-Sea. With kiss-me-quick hats, piers, amusement parks and ice creams the size of traffic cones, it can't be beaten for a fun day out. Southend's pièce de résistance is undoubtedly its seven miles of sandy beaches, but there are plenty of other things to enjoy too: an original Victorian cliff lift has been clanking its way up 57 feet from the promenade to Prittlewell Square since 1912, and the pleasure pier is the longest in the world, reaching 1.34 miles out into the Thames estuary. Heaps of ice cream flavours can be found at longstanding Rossi's ice cream parlour on Marine Parade and the nearby amusement park (pictured left) features more than 60 rides, of which one was voted the most thrilling rollercoaster in the UK by children's TV show *Blue Peter*. There is plenty to do away from the town's nostalgic seafront too; the pier's mile-long railway line takes visitors not to a traditional end-of-the-pier show, but to the Royal Pavilion, a swanky arts centre where concerts and exhibitions are regularly held. The Pavilion's café terrace is also terrific for gazing out to sea. If this inspires some more quiet contemplation, you can always get away from the crowds with a cycle ride to peaceful Shoeburyness (roughly six miles to the east) or the quietly appealing Leigh-on-Sea (three miles to the west, see overleaf) – the boatyards and cockle sheds here will make you feel you're a long way from the bling and bombast of both the big city and the seaside crowds.

—

Get there: *Trains run direct from London Liverpool Street, taking around one hour.*

❖ TWO TREE ISLAND NATURE RESERVE

The 640 acres of mudflats, lagoons and salt marshes of this estuary island (just three miles from Southend) can be accessed via a bridge from Leigh-on-Sea. It's a top birdwatching spot, but even if you're not a 'twitcher', you'll love the sense of tranquility in this remote stretch of marshland.

—

Leigh-on-Sea

www.essexwt.org.uk/reserves/two-tree-island

❖ CANVEY ISLAND

Octagonal, seventeenth-century Dutch cottages, a miniature railway and vintage buses in the Castle Point Transport Museum (Point Road) make Canvey Island a true treasure trove on Essex's coast. Pop to the Heritage Centre (Canvey Road) housed in a former church to learn something of the history of the island, which stretches back to Roman times, and then head to The Labworth Restaurant, designed by Ove Arup in 1932, for lunch and panoramic views of the Thames estuary.

—

www.canveyisland.org

❖ MODEL BOAT LAKE IN SOUTHCHURCH PARK

Set just back from Southend's seafront, Southchurch Park has grassy gardens that are just right for a picnic, particularly if you're not keen on getting sand in your sandwiches... But its main draw is a brilliant model boating lake – bring your own boat and have a go or sit back and watch the enthusiasts do their skilful thing.

—

Kensington Road, SS1 2XA.
01702 420890
www.smpbc.co.uk

❧ BELFAIRS WOODLAND CENTRE

This ancient semi-natural woodland in Leigh-on-Sea is a nature-lover's dream. There's a children's playground and restaurant in the wider park, and more active visitors can take their pick from bowling, tennis, football, cricket and basketball, or book horse and pony rides at nearby Belfairs Riding School (Belfairs Park).

—

Eastwood Road North, Leigh-on Sea, SS9 4LR.
01702 477467
www.essexwt.org.uk/reserves/belfairs

COUNTLESS PEOPLE HAVE EATEN HERE AND GONE ON TO LEAD A NORMAL LIFE

❖ BILLY HUNDREDS

Southend-on-Sea might be all about cockles and whelks, but at Billy Hundreds you're just as likely to get Cornish sardines, boquerones, homemade fishcakes and paella. And while the food's good, you go to Billy for the views. Slap-bang on the beach, it's undoubtedly the best pitch in Southend (if the weather holds out...)

—

Unit 12 Eastern Esplanade, SS1 2YH.
01702 808350
www.billyhundreds.com

BRIGHTON

People have been coming to Brighton on day trips for more than a century and in 2014 it was found to be the most popular UK seaside destination for foreign tourists – a fact presumably related less to the city's supposed invention of the 'dirty weekend' and more to the numerous trains that run from London. With a huge shingle beach just a ten-minute walk from the station alongside numerous other sites and attractions, it's easy to see why this Sussex spot has become a firm favourite. The spectacular mock-Mughal Royal Pavilion, built by John Nash as a seaside retreat for George IV, is the most obvious, but hundreds of smaller pleasures can be found in the North Laine – an old labyrinthine quarter of the city that's home to more than 400 quirky independent shops. You could easily spend the entire day in this warren of tiny streets, but then you'd miss the spirited seafront (pictured left), one that's as traditional as they come and home to some of the city's best eateries. A hearty fish and chip lunch can be found in the ale-battered cod from The Dorset (28 North Road), or grab an ice cream from Marrocco's (8 King's Esplanade); this Brighton institution has been churning up a variety of flavours at its Hove seafront site since 1969. Jack & Linda Mills Traditional Fish Smokers on Kings Road also makes a mean hot mackerel sandwich and it's frequented mostly by locals, though you might have to share with those savvy foreign tourists these days.

—

Get there: *Direct trains run frequently from a number of London stations, taking between 50 and 90 minutes.*

❧ SNOOPERS PARADISE

Ideal for a rainy day, this little indoor market accessed via a tiny turnstile consists of two floors – a ground-floor space selling vintage and antique homeware, accessories, bric-à-brac and 'stuff', as well as a first-floor space predominantly given over to Snoopers Attic, an independent makers' vintage boutique.

———

7–8 Kensington Gardens, North Laine, BN1 4AL.
01273 602558
www.snoopersattic.co.uk

❖ i360

Brighton has lots of quirky places to drink, but this one will literally rise above the crowd. The observation tower by Marks Barfield Architects (designers of the London Eye) will feature the world's first vertical cable car, whizzing 162 metres up a 'vertical pier' to reach a sky bar with fabulous views over the old West Pier.

———

Lower Kings Road Arches, BN1 2LN.
0333 772 0360
www.brightoni360.co.uk

❖ FABRICA

Visual arts organisation Fabrica made the Holy Trinity Church its home almost 20 years ago and has been hosting contemporary art exhibitions here ever since. Large scale visual installations are tailored specifically to make the most of a unique and dramatic space (complete with wrought iron columns) and the results are extraordinary.

———

40 Duke Street, BN1 1AG.
01273 778646
www.fabrica.org.uk

OZZY EGGLETTE

Bacon, FR Egg, Sun-blushed
Tomato & Pesto

£2.70

✤ CAFÉ COHO

With two locations (the other at 83A Queen Street), cute Café Coho has built up an army of fans willing to testify to its cosy ambience, high grade coffee and delicious snacks. The rustic space is set over two floors and offers a wide range of prize-winning produce, local ales and an unusual selection of soft drinks.

—

53 Ship Street, BN1 1AF.
07787 512986
www.cafecoho.co.uk

✤ SHOREHAM AERODROME

This 1930s aerodrome captures the glamour of a bygone age with a Grade II-listed terminal that's an art deco gem. Should it inspire a quick trip to a more glamorous destination there are scheduled flights to France, but if you've forgotten your passport, pleasure flights and flying lessons are also available.

—

Cecil Pashley Way, Shoreham-by-Sea, BN43 5FF.
01273 467373
www.flybrighton.com

HYTHE

The stretch of Kent coast from Hythe to Dungeness is one of the most alluring and surreal in England. Here lie huge concrete discs used as early radar devices in the First World War, squat Martello towers standing guard like redundant ancient sentinels along the coast, houses made of black neoprene, old train carriages converted into homes, fun fairs that look like 1950s throwbacks and a vast shingle spit that is often described as a desert. Hythe, the easiest point to access by rail, is characterised by a tangle of streets filled with antique and vintage shops backing the far-reaching coastline and Fisherman's Beach. Between Hythe and Rye to the west lies the 28-mile-long Royal Military Canal, which offers a number of towpath cycle and walking routes as well as the opportunity for a canal cruise. North of Hythe, Brockhill Country Park and Saltwood Castle, the one-time home of the notoriously rakish MP Alan Clark (buried on its grounds), also make for some scenic walks, but to really get the best from the area opt for an aerial view. From Lydd Airport (www.lyddaero.co.uk), a half an hour flight over the coastline, sweeping over the tiny churches and pubs interspersed among the lakes and fields of Romney Marsh, costs just £84 for one or £105 for three passengers. You even get to have a go at flying the plane.

—

Get there: *Trains run from London St Pancras International and London Charing Cross to Sandling, two miles away, taking between one hour and 90 minutes. From there, the number 18 bus runs to Hythe.*

❖ ST LEONARD'S CHURCH

In keeping with this area's otherwordly feel, the crypt of St Leonard's – a hilltop church dating from the twelfth century – is filled with over 1,000 skulls and other bones from some 4,000 people (supposedly Hythe residents). All are neatly categorised and stacked in a space that's both surprisingly moving and wonderfully memorable.

—

Oak Walk, CT21 5DN.
01303 266217
www.stleonardschurchhythekent.org

❖ THE ROMNEY, HYTHE & DYMCHURCH RAILWAY TO DUNGENESS

This tiny line – a fifteen-inch gauge railway featuring one-third scale steam and diesel locomotives and open-air carriages – connects Hythe with Dungeness, thirteen miles away. En route you're treated to extensive views of Romney Marsh and the RSPB nature reserve. Explore the latter after admiring Dungeness's lighthouses and snacking at the railway café.

---

www.rhdr.org.uk

❖ HYTHE'S HIGH STREET

This shoppers' heaven includes vintage wear at Pixie of Hythe (36), appealing art at Church Mouse Studio (112A) and stationery bliss at ArtWrite (90A). The second-hand furniture at Auntie Wainwright's (53A) could reveal a G Plan gem and the artisan chocolates of Hendricks of Hythe (119) are to die for. For a break, the pastries at La Patisserie of Hythe (116–118) or perfect chips from Torbay of Hythe (81) are, well, perfect.

❖ THE POTTING SHED

This converted corner caff doesn't look like much from the outside but its retro interior houses a microbrewery where you'll find local ales, a decent range of ciders and wines and friendly staff. Take a pew on the small patio area outside if it's a warm day. For a more traditional pub garden, head to the canalside Duke's Head (9 Dymchurch Road).

—

160A High Street, CT21 5JR.
07780 877226

❖ HYTHE BAY SEAFOOD RESTAURANT

For a real seaside treat of super-fresh fish dishes served on a seafront with far-reaching views, this is definitely the place to head. For a lighter meal, fishmonger Griggs of Hythe (Fisherman's Landing Beach, Range Road) turns fresh produce into mouth-watering snacks. The scallop and bacon rolls are made for devouring at one of its brunch tables on the beach.

—

Marine Parade, CT21 6AW.
01303 233844
www.hythebay.co.uk

BROCKENHURST

Brockenhurst's main claims to fame are its mention in the Domesday Book and, more recently, being named the New Forest's largest village in terms of population. But these two bold facts give no insight into just how lovely this day-trip destination is. To truly appreciate its beauty you have to spend some time here and let the special atmosphere weave its spell; it might be the sight of a wild pony wandering at will down Brookley Road, or a deer glimpsed in the woodland, or donkeys grazing on the green, or the dazzling display of rhododendrons blooming along Rhinefield Ornamental Drive in the spring. It's as though the boundaries between the natural world and village life have broken down in Brockenhurst to create a haven for both animals and humans, thanks in no small part to the winding – and often overflowing – stream that runs through the heart of the village. It's not unusual to see cows wandering through the flooded streets, but the stream has its upsides too; just out of town, outside the Balmer Lawn Hotel, it borders a small, sandy beach known as Brockenhurst Beach. To explore it all and discover the heart of the New Forest, hire a bike and get away from the crowds on 100 miles of traffic-free cycle paths.

—

Get there: *Trains run direct from London Waterloo, taking around 90 minutes.*

❖ COUNTRY LANES BIKE HIRE

A huge range of bikes is available to hire here, including mountain bikes, electric bikes and tandems, along with trailers and tag-a-longs. All bike hires include use of a safety helmet, lock and key. The team are friendly and can provide a range of local cycle route maps that begin from the cycle centre, which is located in a restored railway carriage just outside the station.

Brockenhurst Railway Station, SO42 7TW.
01590 622627
www.countrylanes.co.uk

❖ ST NICHOLAS' CHURCH

This sweet Anglican church is just as interesting on the outside as it is on the inside. The churchyard is home to the grave of famous local snake catcher Harry 'Brusher' Mills whose headstone tells his story. It also houses 106 First World War soldiers, most of them New Zealanders from the No.1 New Zealand General Hospital that was stationed here from 1916–19.

Church Lane, SO42 7UB.
01590 624584
www.brockenhurstchurch.com

✤ SETLEY RIDGE VINEYARD & FARM SHOP

Pick up supplies for a lunch at this oak-framed farm shop and plant nursery, which sells a wide range of products sourced as much as possible from within 30 miles, as well as five wines produced at its vineyards. Alternatively, you can sit back and relax in its very own tea room.

Lymington Road, SO42 7UF.
01590 624682
www.setleyridge.co.uk

❖ THE FILLY INN

There are many reasons to choose this cheerful whitewashed pub over worthy competitors such as the nearby Rose & Crown and The Forester Arms. Among them are the lovely garden terrace and its large swathes of outdoor seating and the locally sourced modern British ingredients and well kept beers, which you can enjoy in one of many cosy nooks and crannies nestled within its traditional wood-beamed interior.

Lymington Road, Setley, SO42 7UF.
01590 623449
www.thefillyinn.co.uk

❖ THE PIG RESTAURANT & HOTEL

Brockenhurst has a surprising number of eateries for such a small place, but for an excellent meal in a dappled forest setting, the rustic Pig – just a mile outside the village – is the bee's knees. The food is made from a combination of vegetables grown in The Pig's own walled garden and other produce sourced within 25 miles, and all is served in a gorgeous, faux-Victorian greenhouse dining room. If you overdo it, you can always stay overnight.

—

Beaulieu Road, SO42 7QL.
01590 622354
www.thepighotel.com

BEKONSCOT MODEL VILLAGE

It can be hard to convince the more cynical Londoner just how delightful Bekonscot Model Village & Railway can be, or how it can be quite so absorbing for quite so long, but the 1.5-acre development really does keep visitors hooked for hours. Sat in the heart of Beaconsfield, the oldest model village in the world comprises more than 200 lovingly maintained buildings and up to ten trains running along 450 metres of railway track. It began life as a model railway designed by Roland Callingham who was reputedly told by his wife that either the ever-expanding indoor hobby left the house or she did... Since then, it has grown to encompass a racecourse, boating lake, coalmine, fairground, port, aerodrome and castles. Originally moving with the times to incorporate new models of trains, cars and planes, the decision was made in 1992 to stop modernising and represent the scene as a predominantly 1930s one, and that is how it remains today. It's the detail that makes Bekonscot so special; the gardens of concisely trimmed everyday garden plants, the carefully painted bathers surrounding the lido and the miniature shops with their terrible puns for names. Examining the details of the six towns that now comprise Bekonscot, your eye is constantly drawn by some new and often hilarious aspect, making for a properly grand day out.

—

Bekonscot Model Village, Warwick Road, Beaconsfield, Buckinghamshire, HP9 2PL.
01494 672919, www.bekonscot.co.uk

Get there: *Trains run from London Marylebone to Beaconsfield, taking around 25 minutes. From there, it's a short walk to the model village.*

❖ DORNEYWOOD GARDEN

Just over five miles from Bekonscot, the National Trust's Dorneywood Garden offers horticultural enthusiasts a ramble through a traditional 1930s garden complete with lily pond and stunning herbaceous border – the undoubted star of the show. It's only open on certain days of the summer and is very popular, so book ahead if you're planning a trip.

—

Dorneywood, Dorney Wood Road, Burnham, SL1 8PY.
0844 8001895
www.nationaltrust.org.uk/dorneywood-garden

❖ HOLTSPUR BOTTOM BUTTERFLY RESERVE

For a more rustic encounter with the natural world, the Holtspur Butterfly Reserve just west of Beaconsfield (pictured left) covers eleven acres of meadowland geared towards creating the optimum habitat for butterflies and moths. If you're lucky, you might sight up to 27 species of butterfly, while information boards dotted around will help identify the ones you spot.

—

Riding Lane, Holtspur, near Beaconsfield, HP9 1BT.
www.holtspurbottom.info

❖ THE ROYAL STANDARD OF ENGLAND

This 900-year-old alehouse is the oldest free house in England and as winsome as you'd imagine. Its atmospheric space is dominated by ancient gnarled oak beams overhead, worn flagstones below and, of course, a roaring fire and cosy benches in between. A strong selection of ales and ciders and super-friendly staff put the icing on the cake.

—

Forty Green, Beaconsfield, HP9 1XS.
01494 673382
www.rsoe.co.uk

❖ BENEDICT'S STORE

Pretty little Benedict's, with its pavement tables outside and charming retro inside is one of those places that's likely to please everybody. A broad selection of sandwiches and salads is accompanied by artisan coffees and a delicious range of homemade cakes. And there's also a small, well-chosen selection of locally sourced produce and deli items.

---

12 Gregories Road, Beaconsfield, HP9 1HQ.
01494 678165
www.benedictsstore.co.uk

✤ A WALK ROUND BEACONSFIELD

The market town of Beaconsfield is a lot of fun to explore, not least for the chance to identify and compare real Georgian, neo-Georgian and Tudor revival buildings to their model-village counterparts (pictured above). If any of them look familiar, it's probably because you've seen them on screen: the town has starred in multiple films and TV shows including *Brief Encounter*, *Thunderball*, *Midsomer Murders* and *Hot Fuzz*.

LAVENHAM
p10

DLEY END HOUSE & GARDENS
p16

Sudbury

Ipswich

Braintree

Colchester

MERSEA ISLAND
p104

Chelmsford

Basildon

SOUTHEND & AROUND
p168

Dartford

ROCHESTER
p130

MARGATE
p136

dge

Watfo

High
Wycombe

HENLEY-ON-THAMES

p78

Reading

HAMPTON COU

Marlborough

Newbury

COWORTH PARK p110

p1

RHS WISLEY p72

Guildford

WATERCRESS LINE

p148

Ho

Southampton

ARUNDEL

BROCKENHURST

GOODWOOD p98

p34

p186

p92

BAILIFFSCOURT HOTEL &

LONDON

Dartford

p124
CHISLEHURST CAVES

Croydon

WHITSTABLE

p86

Canterbury

TUDELEY CHURCH

p22

Ashford

p54

SISSINGHURST

p180

HYTHE

wley

p60

RYE

IGHTON

p66   LEWES

p174

p28

HASTINGS

INDEX

Frances Lincoln Limited
A subsidiary of Quarto Publishing Group UK
74–77 White Lion Street
London N1 9PF

Escape London
Copyright © Frances Lincoln 2016
Text copyright © Yolanda Zappaterra
Photographs copyright © Kim Lightbody
Except the following: p.45 left, p.64, p.113 left © Alamy; p.52
© Epping Forest District Museum; p.83 left © River & Rowing
Museum; p.111 © Coworth Park; p.113 right © Royal Ascot; p.118
© Le Manoir aux Quat'Saisons; p.142, p.144 © Historic Royal Palaces;
p.148 © Mid Hants Railway Watercress Line; p.177 © Fabrica.

Design: Sarah Allberrey
Editor: Anna Watson
Commissioning editor: Zena Alkayat

A catalogue record for this book is available from the British Library.

ISBN 978-0-7112-3691-2

Printed and bound in China

9 8 7 6 5 4 3 2

*Front cover: Hythe Beach. Back cover: Magdalen Bridge in Oxford (top),
Anne of Cleves House in Lewes (left) and Hastings High Street (right).
Opening page: the road to Ashwell. p.2 beach huts in Littlehampton;
p.3 a deer grazing in Windsor Great Park; p.4 a bookshop in Lewes;
p.7 Dreamland in Margate; p.8 the Cathedral in Arundel; p.46 Ripley
Nurseries & Farm Shop; p.84 Old Neptune in Whitstable; p.122
the Road Dahl Museum & Story Centre in Great Missenden; p.160
Bekonscot Model Railway Village in Beaconsfield; p.208 Sundae
Sundae in Whitstable. Opposite: the changing of the guard in Windsor.*

Quarto is the authority on a wide range of topics.

Quarto educates, entertains and enriches the lives of
our readers – enthusiasts and lovers of hands-on living.

www.QuartoKnows.com